WHAT READERS ARE SAYING...

"Everyone either has an Aunt Kris or needs one—stat! Her powerful advice and get-ahead ingredients are instinctively digestible, and served in dollops of witty yet tasty bites of pure brilliance. If you feel you are stuck in a rut, step into Ms. Williams' kitchen for some down-home, common-sense morsels of inspiration that will unlock your potential to achieve your most ambitious objectives."

David Glickman, Ultra Mobile, CEO

"Kristin is a world-class leader whose words of wisdom will resonate with everyone. This book is a true testament to her character and the influence she has on many lives, including mine. The stories are relevant and relatable, and provide great solutions and tips for any young professional who is unsure of who they are, or who they should be professionally. The sincerity and honesty of her words are timeless."

**Melanie Evidente Zeiss, Living Spaces,
Manager of Training Systems and Content**

"Aunt Kris has whipped up a hearty serving of timeless wisdom in a way that our generation can easily apply to our professional and personal lives. Take a seat at Kristin's table and get your fill of practical stories that have risen from generations of life lessons and will leave you feeling stuffed!"

**Michael Smith, K-dub (a.k.a. Aunt Kris)
Mentee and Founder of Yip Yap**

"*Aunt Kris, Can You Help Me* is a MUST read for millennials! Kristin Williams provides sage advice in this engaging narrative to equip those newer to the workforce with the tools necessary to be successful in today's market. Her 10 ingredients make the perfect recipe for success. Through the book's relatable vignettes, which blend generous helpings of wisdom, humor, real-world experience and the aromas of delicious food, Aunt Kris' recipe is a blue-ribbon winner for personal and professional success!"

Sandra Bulgin, former Head of Staffing and Recruitment, Farmers Insurance Group

"This terrific book takes storytelling as a teaching tool to a new level. Everyone, young and old, learns from a well-told story! The stories from her life and the examples provided from the young professionals are perfect, as they guide the reader to new ideas about themselves and their careers. A quick read, with easy suggestions, to take careers to the next level."

Jan Slater, JanSlater.net, Founder

"Where was this book when I was young? Aunt Kris has such a way of coaching through real-life situations, you truly feel the caring touch a family member would provide. I loved that Aunt Kris even included the mentees' outcomes of her coaching—the emotions are priceless!"

Wendy Weeks, Youth Employment Service (YES), Executive Director

Aunt Kris,
Can You Help Me?

10 INGREDIENTS
for Career and Life Success
as a Young Professional

Kristin Williams
MNK Engagement, LLC

Aunt Kris, Can You Help Me?

10 Ingredients for Career and Life Success as a Young Professional

Published by
MNK Engagement LLC
Huntington Beach, California

www.AuntKris.com

Cover & Interior Illustration by Avanese Yuvienco
Cover Design by Dan Mulhern Design

Interior Design by Dawn Teagarden

ISBN: 978-1983427145

Printed in the United States of America

www.AuntKris.com

To the Love of My Life…
Trapping you was the single best decision I ever made.

ACKNOWLEDGMENTS
HOW BLESSED AM I?
LET ME COUNT
THE WAYS...

TO THE GUIDING presence that is my mother's wisdom, thank you for sustaining me and the energy of this project.

To My Family...

To my siblings, Shelley, John, Kippy, Rick, and Laura. I acknowledge that while we share the same biological parents, the experiences they had in raising you informed their approach in raising me, and I am the better for it. They say you can't pick your family, but I seriously don't think I could have done better if I'd had the chance.

To my amazing husband, Em. I will honor your desire for no PDA, and trust that you know I am aware of the fact that you do "everything around here."

To my parents, who were truly in love. Being the youngest, I benefited from more time and witness of your kind affection to one another. You taught me what is truly important in a relationship.

Your love not only produced six children, but eighteen grandkids and seventeen great grandkids, which I have affectionately named Neubauer Nation! Thank you for never tampering my dreams or my independent spirit.

To my mother-in-law. Thank you for raising the steward of my heart. When I met you the first time, I realized why he was so comfortable with a strong woman; it was not a foreign experience.

To my niece and nephews across the pond. Thank you for loving your American auntie; it's a joy to watch your growing families.

To All of My Mentees and Coaches...

To my early group of mentees, Aubrey, Miranda, Melanie, Mike "Boots", and Joe "Slaughter". You may not have asked for my advice, but you understood my intention was honest. I am always thrilled no matter how much time has passed to hear how you are doing. You have each enriched my life along this journey and helped me affirm that this story needed to be told.

To my mentees who lovingly call me MaMa HAM (hard ass mom). You know who you are and how much we have achieved. May the success you have achieved during our tenure allow you to mentor a young professional later in your career.

To Jan Slater, the best coach and mentor I could ever be fortunate enough to know. Your generosity over the years has truly added to the fabric of my life. Thank you for keeping me real.

To My Team...

To Amanda Johnson, thank you for your patience. Who knew this journey would take as long as it did. You never wavered or allowed me to do so. Thank you for "getting it" and asking the critical questions that shaped this story. Your fingerprints are lovingly all over this project. Our brief encounter and introduction has grown into an amazing partnership for which I am eternally grateful. What's next? Who knows, but I know it will be a great ride.

To Aubrey, thank you for bringing your unabashed enthusiasm to my work every day. For being the best support system. This journey has only begun, and I can't think of anyone better to organize my events and be at my side. I also can't thank you enough for asking the critical cooking questions, such as: "What makes pesto green... jalapeño?" You bring fun and laughter to everything you do!

To Dan Mulhern and Avanese Yuvienco, for diving in full force with your XCEL team. From book cover design to website and more, I am certain you have magical powers.

To Kathy Sparrow and Alyssa Coelho, for making sure it was powerful and polished enough to go to print. Your editing and insights are a blessing to me, and to all the young professionals who will benefit from your contribution. Thank you!

With All My Love and Gratitude,

Aunt Kris

CONTENTS

INTRODUCTION
AUNT KRIS, WHAT AM I MISSING?

SITTING AT A marble high-top bistro table at the Fairmont Hotel, I enjoyed a cup of coffee while I waited for her to arrive. We worked on different coasts, and this technology conference had opened the opportunity for some good face-to-face time. I could tell from her voice on the phone the other night that this was not going to be our typical "let's catch up" meeting.

What did she mean—she feels stuck and doesn't know what to do? I wondered as I sipped my hot drink and set it down on the table.

I looked up just as she arrived and waved her over. She smiled and greeted me on her way to the table, and jumped into conversation before setting her burgundy briefcase on the floor.

"Kristin, I feel like I am stuck in life. I am not moving forward, and I fear I may even be slipping. Work is not moving ahead, and I've been dating Ben for five years and there is still no talk of marriage. My clock is ticking, and I don't want to miss the opportunity to have a family." She looked down at the steaming coffee the waitress had placed in front of her and sighed, obviously trying to hold tears back.

Whoa, I wonder how long this video of doom has been playing in her head?

"Cate, slow down. Let's order breakfast and talk through this." I met her glistening eyes with a smile and waved the waitress over.

Good food makes any problem a little easier to solve.

Over the next hour, we talked through each issue that had my mentee paralyzed in perpetual motion and came up with a game plan. She realized she needed to be more intentional about her Personal Brand (chapter one), look at options she hadn't considered before (chapter three), and figure out the balance in her relationship (chapter five).

As we unpacked and strategized, I watched her face soften, her shoulders relax, and her posture straighten.

There's the brilliant, capable person I know her to be.

She glanced at the clock and, realizing it was time to get back to her conference, waved the waitress over for the check. After paying, she gave me a quick hug and turned to walk out of the bar.

Suddenly, she stopped and turned around to ask, "Kristin, how do you know all this? I've been wrestling with this for weeks, and you had insights that made it really clear for me in a matter of minutes. Where did that come from?"

"My mom." I smiled as memories of my mom floated across my mind.

"Wow, she must be an amazing woman…" she smiled back.

"Yes, she was…I owe much of my success to her," I nodded and watched her nod in understanding and head back to her conference.

My relationship with my mom and the wisdom she imparted to me was clearly unique. How many other young professionals are struggling because they are missing ingredients that my mom poured into me?

It breaks my heart and infuriates me when I hear someone in the media distill the issues millennials face in the workplace to "being or acting entitled." In my opinion, that's just an easy, inexperienced soundbite to describe their perceived problem.

Don't they have young people in their lives? Of course, but their sons, daughters, nieces, and nephews aren't like that. It's everyone else.

But let's be real about this right now.

If you are reading this book, it's not because you feel entitled—it's because you're sincerely looking for the skills and advice you didn't get in school or from the adults in your life. Plus, you were raised during an era of technological communication that probably made you a fantastic problem-solver, but left you at a deficit when it comes to communicating face-to-face in a manner that builds trust and rapport.

You are just as brilliant and capable as your elders—you're just missing an ingredient or two. You don't know what you don't know, but you do know that what you're currently doing isn't getting you noticed and helping you get ahead.

And that's why I wrote this book for you.

What I have found in all of my years of mentoring is that young professionals like you devour new information. You want to be developed. You desire to learn and grow. You are open to trying new things, but you need a little help understanding what those new things are.

Having mentored hundreds of young professionals just like you, I have more hope for the future than I ever have. I think of the rate of technology advancement from my mother's generation to mine, and now to the next generation, and I believe you are anything but entitled.

In fact, I believe you have an inherent fairness factor, and that as you rise to levels of power, it will serve you and our society well. I believe you are capable of creating solutions that the generations before you could not or would not solve when we had the chance.

All you need is a little guidance from someone who has been there and done that. For the last thirty plus years in sales, management, and human resources, I have acquired tacit knowledge that can only be gained through experience, and I want to share with you what I learned.

After years of sharing my stories of succeeding despite the challenges of that era with young professionals, and seeing firsthand the success they achieved with a trusted resource and mentor, I knew I had to write a book and launch AuntKris.com to help all of the young professionals like you, who want to get noticed, get ahead, and whip up success in their lives.

I've experienced success in technology, media, research, and wireless industries; but I have watched my blood and professionally adopted nieces and nephews adapt what they've learned from me into their industries.

And I look forward to hearing from you, as you learn and add each key ingredient to your own personal and professional life and whip up your own success.

HOW TO READ THIS BOOK

Blending my love for mentoring with my love for good food has been fun, and you'll find that each chapter addresses one of the ingredients every young professional needs to get noticed and get ahead.

I've shared stories from my early years as a young professional, and how my mom's wisdom guided me through some very challenging situations. By the way, these stories are representative of true events, but some of the details—including names, titles, and locations—have been changed.

I recommend that you give yourself time to digest each chapter. Maybe grab a journal and take some notes about ways to add these ingredients into your professional career.

I'm excited you're here. I know that you may be feeling very overwhelmed at the moment, but trust me when I tell you that this is not rocket science. The ingredients are simple, but potent enough to quickly change the flavor of your life.

Also, please feel free to contact me at www.AuntKris.com if you have questions or need additional resources.

CHAPTER ONE
MY MOM + MADONNA

AS I PULLED THE glass door open, I saw my young mentee slumped over in a booth in the corner of the coffee shop.

Oh yeah, she looks pretty frustrated.

Walking up to her, I noticed this bright twenty-five-year-old's furrowed brow and the tension in her hands as she gripped her cell phone. Dressed in a black skirt and red silk blouse, her expression told me she felt everything but successful despite her "dressed for success" attire.

Relief washed over her face when she noticed me slipping into the booth, and she started in the moment I sat down on the cool, comfy leather seat.

"Aunt Kris, thank you for agreeing to meet me. I know you're busy so I will get to the point. I want to get ahead at work, but my boss is not receptive. I have a new idea on how to save money, but if he won't listen, we won't see the cost savings. Can you help?"

Looking into her troubled green eyes, I smiled. "Absolutely. What's your PBI?" I glanced over at the counter, hoping the line would shorten soon. The freshly baked croissants were calling my name.

"My PBI? What's that?" She shook her head and her blonde curls bounced on her shoulders.

"Oh, sorry. That's my shorthand for Personal Brand Intention. Whether you know it or not, you have a brand. If you are not driving your brand/image, it is being assigned to you. *Every* action or inaction sends a message to others in the workplace. Every interaction allows you to add or detract from your brand. There is no 'neutral.' You have to be intentional to make sure the brand you have is the brand you want." I searched her face to make sure she was tracking with me.

Yeah, she gets it.

Glancing at the still-long line again, I decided to launch into the heart of the conversation and make sure she understood PBI. "Think about your workplace. I'm going to describe some people, and I want you to see if you recognize any of these characters."

I took a sip of the coffee she had purchased for me and then dove into my descriptions.

"Grace the Gossiper: The one who is always talking about others at work, sharing personal tidbits.

"Wade the Workaholic: He may not work smart, but he works long hard hours. That may get him ahead for a while until he burns out or, worse, people start to see that as incompetence.

"Cameron the Quietly Competent: Just gets the work done, and does not socialize much.

"Oscar the Over-Sharer: Always sharing far too much personal information.

"Debbie Drama: You know, the one who over-exaggerates, so her ideas and comments are dismissed easily.

"You see where I'm going, right? These people have brands that grow out of the traits for which they are most known."

Smiling in understanding, the young lady in front of me finished a sip of her steaming hot cocoa, "I totally get it. Yes, we have some of those characters where I work."

"When I was twenty-six and had been in a sales career for a little more than four years, I learned the importance of driving your brand intentionally, and it paid off big time…"

Why do I feel so anxious?

Sitting at the desk in my home office, a small corner of my bedroom in the apartment, I noticed that I was gripping my pen with a little extra fervor and my shoulders were up near my ears.

Up until that moment, I was so excited to return to the publication that started my career and flattered that they had fought so hard to get me back into a new role on the sales team. It had been less than two years since they so easily let me go to the competition, but I felt no bitterness. Heck, I wouldn't have offered me that senior of a position given my experience at the time, but the competition took a risk and it paid off. In the interim, I built a reputation of exceeding sales goals (year 1–190% of quota) and building strong relationships with clients. I had arrived and made a statement; and with my new track record, my old publication engaged me to take on the role of coordinating sales for a national insert into our magazine. If successful, it could become its own publication.

Staring at my death-grip on my pen, I asked myself again, *Why am I feeling so anxious?* And then, I flashed on a recent conversation with a colleague.

What she said must still be bothering me.

A good friend of mine, who worked in the East Coast office where I would be working soon, called to tell me what was being said about me. "Everyone is nervous you are coming to call on their clients. They don't want you here because they think you can't handle it."

"What do you mean they think I can't handle it?"

I really was a bit surprised.

Who is saying this? The sales leadership must have thought I could do it. They asked me to come back after all.

Then I started feeling angry. Really angry. And because I had let my angry, razor-sharp tongue get me in trouble before, I worked hard to control my breathing and tone. I was glad it was a phone conversation, as I could feel the heat rising in my face and the tension in my body increasing.

Of course, it didn't matter. My friend could tell how upset I was and started dialing back on what she had said. "Kristin, it's no big deal. All sales people are territorial. That's probably all this is. You know you're from California, not here."

My temper was pretty wild. Feeling the anger beginning to take over and knowing I was on the brink of an explosion, I abruptly ended the call to calm down.

That was a few days ago, but it's still bothering me.

I closed my eyes to fight back tears of anger. The TV was dialed into a major news network, and I let the lull of the broadcaster's voice serve as "white noise" so I could focus on my breathing.

While the curtains were still pulled, I heard the apartment gardeners working below. My thoughts drifted to nature, and I noticed my breathing returning to normal. I sat there, almost motionless, trying to release the tension in my muscles.

Suddenly, I knew what I had to do.

California Girl, huh? I'll show them.

As the tension began to lift, my thoughts drifted to the day I had proven to my mom that I had learned this lesson.

It was the last day of second grade and I was super excited. My mom knew I had to look my best. It was a special day, but not because I was about to go to the third grade. It was special because I was allowed to carry the family camera to school. At the end of the day, I was going to get a picture taken with my teacher, Mrs. Frost. I loved Mrs. Frost. She didn't scold me too often for talking in class like other teachers did. Instead, she just asked me to do something different. She also had the whitest hair I had ever seen. It was white like snow with a smooth texture that reminded me of Mrs. Claus.

When school ended, I went to get my picture with Mrs. Frost. We were outside the door of our classroom on the sidewalk, and I took my camera out of its pouch and handed it to another teacher who was going to snap the picture. But when I turned around with a huge smile, and looked at Mrs. Frost, I froze.

Oh no. That's not okay.

I dashed into action as I screamed, "Stay here. I will be right back." Thankfully, my house was across the street from my school. I ran as fast I could, barreling through the door so loudly that my mom yelled, "What's going on?"

I knew I had to answer, but I also had to act fast.

I will have to answer her questions when I come back.

Before she could stop me, I was in and out of the bathroom in a flash and darting out the front door.

Mrs. Frost and the other teacher were still there waiting for me.

I did it.

Then I gave Mrs. Frost what I ran home for—a hair comb.

My mom had always said the same thing every day as I headed out of the house: "Kristin, you need to look your best and behave if you want to be invited back."

I was so upset when I saw Mrs. Frost's hair ruffled by the Santa Ana wind. I could not allow a photo that I planned to cherish forever to be taken of her looking different than this perfect image I had in my mind.

That's it! I have a brand problem.

I was not sure exactly what "being Californian" meant, but I knew it wasn't good for this situation.

If my co-workers who know me well have this resistance, what will clients think?

"Look your best and behave so you will be invited back." Mom's words floated through my mind again.

That's what I have to do.

It wasn't that I had to change who I was, but I did need to be aware of the image and brand I was projecting and make sure it was not an obstacle to my success.

I would still be "me" during the meetings because my sales style was one characterized by trying to understand what my clients wanted to achieve.

I always make sure to make my intentions clear. Clients and colleagues accept me as soon as they know I only want to help them achieve their goals.

I would still ask questions, listen, and be truthful about what options (my products and services, as well as other choices) they might consider. I never spoke ill of the competition—just stayed with the facts and asked questions so my clients could come to their own conclusion. My "California" customers rewarded me with additional business because of this approach.

My natural style was a good fit with my previous clients, but now I had to learn to appeal to a larger audience.

I obviously had the knowledge and skills to do the job, but I had been completely unaware, up until this moment, how important branding and packaging was to this equation.

It's time for me to act like modern-day brand master Madonna and reinvent myself to retain and grow my fan base in business.

I began to think about what to pack for the trip. I shifted forward in my soft black chair, sitting on the edge. When the wheels almost pushed the chair from underneath me, I regained my balance and, as I did, my attention was captured by the TV. I saw the broadcaster and began to study her look—light grey blouse with a royal blue blazer. Her necklace was silver with a small pendant and stud earrings. Even though her base was in Atlanta, there was no distinctive accent in the tone of her voice. She had to appeal to millions of viewers, and she did this in a way that her personal brand did not detract from the news or stories she wanted her audience to focus on. She was not the story.

The anxiety subsided as the picture became clear. I would pay more attention to the physical image I would project on this trip and how I would handle a meeting. In California, with annual warm weather and a casual lifestyle, bright colors and laid-back social undertones in business meetings were common.

That won't work as well in Boston.

I had been to Boston several times before. I knew the city and had many friends there, so I repacked my suitcase with my new visual brand.

My "banker's suit" was a dark navy skirt and blazer with a silk cream camisole. It said clearly that I was about business. Light silver jewelry would finish the look and prove that I paid attention to details.

I may also have to shift my relaxed style, I thought as I held up the suit to myself in the mirror. I would make sure that my posture and body language told potential clients I was approachable and thoughtful. I would take the lead from my colleague as to the proper seat to take in the offices or conference rooms where we would meet. *There is always a preference or "pecking order" to how people like to sit in meetings. Should I sit across from the client so our conversation can go back and forth like a ping-pong rally? Or do we sit next to each other in a conversational manner like a guest at a dinner table?* Needless to say, I would also have to choose my words carefully, avoiding typical Southern California jargon such as "like," "all," "and," "so," "whatever," and "totally," which are employed as linguistic fillers. I wanted to eliminate the risk of a failed first impression.

A few days later, before leaving my hotel for the office in Boston, I took a second look in the mirror and said, "Behave in a way so you get invited back."

When I entered our office off Boylston Street, the look on my colleagues' faces was priceless. I wished I had a camera. They were stunned.

"Not enough California?" I smiled back at them to let them know it was all good.

Barriers down, we focused on the task at hand—getting advertisers to say "yes" to a new insert publication. I spent the week traveling with different sales reps, pitching the special publication. We worked together to create proposals that offered the most advantages to advertisers who maintained or increased their business with both publications we offered.

The result?

We increased overall spending (which was good for our pay-checks), and we did so at the expense of our competition's market share. The experiment was a financial success for that fiscal year, even though the insert never became its own independent publication.

I noticed the leather had lost its cool touch on the back of my legs. With the temperature warming, I wondered how much time I had left to offer this young woman before I had to leave for a family engagement.

She had been hanging onto my every word, showing me how hungry she was to get ahead and how willing she was to learn how to do it.

This is important. My family will understand if I am a little late to the restaurant.

"I'm confident that my image and brand overhaul was one of the keys in our success. I was specific and intentional when deciding how I wanted to be received. How I showed up visually—my clothing, my posture, my language—all worked together to set my team and future clients at ease from the moment we connected, and that is always a good start to any relationship."

The young woman nodded, her curls bouncing harder than they had when I'd arrived, affirming that she was not only following me, but the frustration and confusion were lifting.

"So, now that you see how focusing on my brand helped me drive my career, you can see the importance of considering what your brand is. What message are you sending? Once you know what your brand currently is, you are well on your way to shaping it."

"What if my brand isn't what I want it to be?" There was a tinge of fear in her voice.

"Well, you can change jobs and start to rebrand yourself, although that could be a drastic move. The simpler approach is to begin to change your behaviors and actions to drive the brand you want in your present circumstances. You don't have to become something you're not. In fact, I don't recommend it. That's not sustainable, and you would quickly become exhausted and unhappy."

"Yes, I think I've seen some of my managers do that." She scrunched her nose to show me how she felt about the choices they had made to be inauthentic.

"That's right. So, the first thing to do is define your brand, and then choose actions and behaviors—that's where intent comes in—that align with the characteristics of your brand or PBI."

"What kind of actions and behaviors?" Her voice quivered.

"Well, it's hard for me to say until I learn more about your job now and what you want to move into. Some common areas to pay attention to are:

Meetings

- Are you on time?
- Do you participate? If yes, do you listen as well as speak up?
- What does your body language say? If you are bored, be careful not to let that show by slouching, doodling, and keeping your head down.
- Do you volunteer for extra assignments as the action items are assigned?

General Appearance

- Even if you have a casual work environment, there may still be truth in the saying, "Dress for the job you want, not the one you have."

- Your workspace—is it cluttered or disorganized? Are the work surfaces clean?

Performance Review

- Do you wait until your company's formal cycle?
- Are you able to ask for a one-on-one meeting with your boss to have an interim review?
  - If yes, it may be a good idea to let him/her know your intentions and ask what additional assignments you might get involved with to learn and grow.
  - If no, then be prepared with discussion points for the formal review cycle."

"Okay, I see what you mean. I guess I really never thought too much about all of that, but now that you point it out, it makes perfect sense."

I heard the relief in her voice and her green eyes were no longer shrouded in fear. "If you can learn to assess while in the moment at work, and make adjustments, you can start to shape your business brand. From there, you can build a case for what YOU offer the company and why they should consider you for advancement."

"Thank you, Aunt Kris! I'm going to get started today." And with a quick hug, she nearly skipped out of the coffee shop beside me.

Six Months Later...

The phone rang and I dug through my handbag quickly, hoping to catch it before it went to voicemail.

"Hello?" I said as I held it up to my ear and sat down at my dining room table.

"Hi, Aunt Kris. Do you have a minute?" The excitement was oozing in her voice.

"Yes, what's up?" Although Caller ID was not available, I knew exactly who it was.

"Well, I wanted to update you on what's happening at work." Her speed was picking up.

"I would love to hear. I think you had a specific idea you wanted to share with your boss, right?"

"That's right. Well, I spent some time really thinking about what you told me when we met. I thought about previous times when I tried to get my boss to pay attention to an idea and maybe why I wasn't successful."

"And what did you determine?" I coaxed.

"Well, it wasn't easy. I think what I learned when I was honest with myself was that my personal brand was being assigned to me. I thought about the characters you described in business and I realized that I was letting Debbie Drama take up a lot of my time at work. You know how I like to be helpful."

"Yes, you do have a way of picking up strays. I remember when you brought home a litter of abandoned puppies."

She groaned. "Please don't remind me. I don't know that Mom has forgiven me yet. Anyway, while I know that I was getting my work done, and I am no Debbie Drama, I can see how my boss may have assigned some of those attributes to me through association."

"Okay, what did you do then?" I asked, pleased at her newly found awareness.

"Well, I didn't abandon Debbie Drama. I did, however, limit our conversations to when we bumped into each other in common areas like the break room. When she would approach me at my desk, I would just ask politely to talk at lunch or on break."

"Well, that sounds like an intentional action and behavior. How did Debbie Drama respond?"

"That's the funny thing. She was fine with it. I guess I thought her approaching me during my workday with non-work-related topics was urgent. That was my fault."

"Well, I wouldn't place blame. It was just you weren't in the moment and assessing the situation like we discussed. Now you know to do that." I tried to encourage her to take responsibility but leave the regret behind.

"That's it. When I thought through how to be intentional and drive my brand, I wanted my boss and his boss to see me as reliable and productive. If they have a less than positive view of someone seen as exaggerating, then maybe I am seen that way and my ideas would not be received with serious consideration."

"Exactly! So how does it end?" Now my excitement was mounting.

"I knew this would take time to change my brand, so I defined what I wanted and kept looking for opportunities to show my personal brand intention."

"And? The suspense is killing me." I laughed.

"When I approached my boss with ideas in the past, I pitched him based on what I thought was important. I had no idea what he felt was important when weighing a decision. So, in a one-on-one meeting, I just asked him. I said, 'Dan, when you are trying to decide on an idea proposed from an employee or a vendor, what do you need to feel that you have all the information to make the best decision?' And he told me. So, I worked within that framework when I presented my cost savings idea. See, I thought it was all about the savings and a slam dunk. However, I learned about the impact to other teams, savings coming at a lower quality solution, and much more."

She is really getting it!

"What happened when you proposed your idea in this framework?"

"Well, I did identify a cost savings of 10%. However, when we went through the process, we came up with a better solution as a team that saves 13%. While my idea ultimately wasn't the best idea, we came up with one and my boss congratulated me for starting the conversation. He said this would be considered during my review.

And I received a raise. By being proactive, I will get to work on more complex projects moving forward. I am so excited!"

I pulled the phone away from my ear, as her excitement had become volume. "That's great. Now just build on what you started and stay intentional about your brand."

"I will. Thanks again!"

I set the phone down and now it was my turn to nearly skip my way back to the kitchen to pull the roast out of the oven.

CHAPTER TWO
THE FAMILY CORPORATION

AS I WALKED FROM the air-conditioned family room into my friend's backyard, the hot summer sun assaulted me. In fact, my dark Prada sunglasses fogged up from the change in temperature while I searched for my young mentee. She had texted me earlier in the day, saying she needed to talk. Taking my sunglasses off, I spotted her in the pool and waved to her.

She smiled and waved, and I found a couple of chairs in the shade while she climbed out of the pool, wringing her dark hair the way you squeeze water from a towel. Still dripping wet, she grabbed two drinks from the cooler before she found a towel and made her way over to me.

Smiling, she stretched her tall, thin body on the open chair next to me, handed me a bottle of water, and dove right into the topic behind her text.

"I was asked to take on a new role at work, but I am not sure I want it." She looked down at the drink in her hands.

"Why don't you think you want it?" A slight breeze picked up, and I glanced at the palm trees' leaves, now gently swaying.

"I am not sure it will put me on a path for further advancement. I joined the company to be exposed to lots of different areas and learn. Now the president and my boss asked me to take a job as a recruiter because I have staffing in my background, but I have already done that."

"Do you know why they need someone?" I asked, turning to face her.

"Because the person doing it left," she answered matter-of-factly and rolled her long, dark hair up, tucking it into a bun.

"Do you know why they asked *you*?" I started to dig for the details we needed.

"What do you mean?" She raised an eyebrow and waited for clarification.

"Well, if the president and your boss came to you and asked you to do this, there must be a reason. And not just the first obvious one you may think of—they also must have confidence that you can do it."

"Well, they did say the company is expecting a lot of growth and that finding the right talent is key to the success of the company." Her head cocked to the side, as if a new possibility was emerging.

"It is true that the right talent is the key to the success of a company, and it's equally important that you know the role and contribution you have there, and really own it. I remember my first job in a corporation and how intimidated I was until I figured out my sweet spot and how I could help my company grow…"

As we opened the car doors to get out, the heat immediately assaulted us—a harsh contrast to the air conditioning in the rental car. It was an exceptionally warm day for June, and the blacktop was so hot that I could feel the heat piercing through the soles of my shoes like sharp blades of fire.

The three of us were huddled in the parking lot of the business complex, strategizing for this meeting, but I was distracted.

Why didn't I just take the extra two minutes to run back into the house to get my sunglasses? I asked myself as I tried hard not to squint. I didn't want to give anyone a reason to doubt they'd made the right hiring decision.

I don't want to do anything to jeopardize this amazing opportunity.

I glanced sideways at my new boss, Oliver, and thought about the day we'd met and the not-so-easy journey of getting this job.

The day on the boat was so relaxing—filled with tons of great conversation, a little limbo dancing, and too much drink and sun.

My boyfriend had invited Oliver on the boat that day, and I had been looking forward to getting to know him after hearing some great things. The boat galley had a bar area that I had set up; and as I stood next to it, I spotted Oliver sitting on a cushioned bench on the side of the boat. I decided to initiate the conversation.

"Oliver, Jay says he met you during a sales call. What do you do exactly?" I smiled up at his tan face and the large, jet-black eyes that matched his hair. Sitting stretched out on one of the white boat cushions, his plaid swim trunks still wet from a swim, I noticed his legs did not get as much sun as his face.

He smiled back and set his drink down. "I work for a technical publication, *Mainframe News*. I started working in the editorial department, but I moved to California to work in sales."

"Why did you change departments? Those seem like very different jobs?" I probed.

"I liked being an editor and living in New York where the business is based. But my family is from Northern California, so I wanted to get back to the West Coast." He paused for another sip of his martini. "Plus, you can make more money in sales."

"That makes sense." I liked him immediately and really enjoyed the rest of our conversation.

Soon after our day on the water, Oliver mentioned to my boyfriend that he needed a sales assistant. My name was offered up for consideration, and Oliver and I started to discuss the possibility. For Oliver, it was a done deal; for the rest of the people who had a say in this decision, it was a different story.

My interview process was a bit contentious because I had not finished my college degree. Even the receptionist had a college degree, and there was a lot of discussion on whether I should even be hired as a sales assistant. I was in school and working full-time, and I really didn't get why that made me "less than" others who had the option to go to school full-time before working.

During the interview, it came up with everyone I spoke with and sometimes more than once. I wanted to scream, "Why are you still talking to me if I am not worthy of this position?" But they kept talking, and I kept my composure somehow. I answered questions like, "What's your five-year plan?" and "What books are you reading right now?" I remember being so exhausted from the mental stress of being "on my game" that even my hair hurt.

But my patience paid off.

"Kristin, you're hired," Oliver said the words with such relief. "I'll see you on Monday."

And there we were, in the parking lot, with the associate publisher, Drew, who I hadn't met during my interview process. Drew was in his mid-forties, with sparkling blue eyes, and the hint of becoming a dashing silver fox. Oliver had told me that he was in town because we were buying the competition and putting them out of business, and I was trying to understand exactly what that meant. I knew we were a computer newspaper, and we sold advertising to people who made computer products. It seemed obvious that with one less magazine, there would be more business for the two newspapers left; but beyond that, I had a lot to learn.

After a brief introduction to Drew and the huddle on the hot asphalt to discuss what we were going to do in the meeting, we made our way to the office building.

Oliver meandered ahead of us, while Drew and I walked toward the elevator with more measured precision. I was enjoying the cool shade of the large tree next to the elevator when a soft touch on my arm grabbed my attention. I looked up at Drew in time to hear him say, "It's your job to make sure this works!" His voice was soft, but it delivered that statement with tons of force.

All I could do was nod at him wide-eyed as the elevator doors opened and we stepped inside.

What does he mean, "It's your job to make this work?" What is "this"?
Before I could process more, I found myself in lockstep, following Drew and Oliver into the office.

The excitement of meeting upper management, purchasing a competitor, and everything else I was looking forward to on my first day had melted away. It felt like the heat of the summer and Drew's comment had conspired to broil uncertainty in my mind.

I so don't know what I am doing today, I thought to myself as we all took our seats around the large conference table. *Kristin, you got this. You can do it. You just need to survive the day. Take it one step at a time. Baby steps, Kristin. Baby steps.* I coached myself before devoting all my attention to the meeting at hand.

The meeting appeared to go well; and over the next 48 hours, when Drew and I had some time to talk, I started to get an idea of what he was trying to tell me by the elevator. He mentioned that Oliver was not his first choice to lead sales for the West Coast, but that his boss and Oliver were good friends from their days in college, which left him feeling uncertain about Oliver and this process of buying out the competition and increasing sales.

"Kristin, we just put sales resources into this region to see if we can grow sales. The competition has a district sales manager and assistant, so we have you and Oliver as our team."

"Drew, I am very honored for the opportunity to be part of the team. I am looking forward to rolling up my sleeves and getting to work."

"Well, this better work, or there will be consequences," he declared.

Holy crap!
As I entered my apartment that evening, my muscles still tense from that intense conversation, all I could think of was getting

my shoes off, pouring a glass of wine, and brainstorming how to "make this work."

What have I gotten myself into?

As I pondered what to do next, I was surprised at the image that popped into my mind.

What does walking home from school with a note pinned to my sweater have to do with starting a job in stressful sales environment?

Before I left school that early fall afternoon, my teacher pinned a note to my sweater and told me to make sure my mom read it.

When the bell rang, I grabbed my things and headed to the crosswalk to await an escort to cross the street. This day we had an older lady who walked to the middle of the street, held up a stop sign, and motioned for us to step off the curb to cross. Despite the disapproving look she gave me, I decided I would skip all the way home to the afternoon treat that I knew was waiting for me.

When I got home, my mom immediately saw the note and removed it from my sweater before cutting me a slice of freshly-baked cinnamon cake. She sat down to read the note, while I ate my cake and watched her. She sat upright, her slender body taking up a small portion of the chair. Her mousy brown hair was set in soft curls from her weekly wash and set, revealing her high cheekbones and bright hazel eyes behind smart glasses. I watched her lips—red, with her favorite lipstick—move subtly as she read the note.

When I got up to fill my glass with water, she asked me for my report card. I pulled out the beige card stock that was folded in half. The cover had the name of the school printed on it and spaces where my teacher printed my name, her name, and the dates of the school year. The first panel had a grid with my subjects (math, reading, art, etc.) listed on the left and then three columns to the right where my teacher would write in my grade for each report period. I usually got A's and B's.

After I finished my snack, my mom said, "Kristin, we need to talk." It didn't feel like the "you're in trouble voice" was being used, but it also was not a tone that represented total satisfaction.

"Kristin, let's look at your report card together. Your teacher has written to tell me of some changes…" We sat down side-by-side at the oval maple kitchen table. When she opened the report card, I immediately saw the column where my grades were listed side by side and then I saw my math grade for this period: C.

It jumped off the page and practically hit me in the face. I didn't really like math, but I couldn't believe I didn't get a B again. Then I looked at the panel to the right, a grid filled almost exclusively with capital S's, and there was a glaring capital U (for Unsatisfactory) in the classroom behavior space.

I wasn't sure what was coming, but I knew it wasn't going to be good.

I have bad grades. Is Mom going to give me the paddle? What is my punishment going to be?

I tried hard to fight back tears. My lip was quivering, and I hung my head down so my mom couldn't see my face.

That's when she spoke. "Kristin, your teacher wrote a note to say that you are a delight in class, but lately you have been talking quite a bit. She thinks this lack of focus is not only why you received a C in math, but also was disruptive to other kids trying to study. That's why she gave you a U in conduct in the classroom. What do you have to say about it?" Her right eyebrow challenged me gently.

"Mom, I know I talk in class, but I didn't think it was that bad." I looked down at the floor.

"Kristin, it's not that it is bad or you are bad—it's about not doing your job the best you can." Her brow relaxed a bit as she leaned back in her chair.

"My job?" I cocked my head to the side. "What job?"

"Kristin, everyone has a role. Your dad's role is to go to work and bring home a paycheck so we can have a home and buy the things we need like food and clothes. Mine is to take care of the home and you kids so you grow up happy and healthy. We should work every day to do our best in performing our roles, so we don't let ourselves down and so that the family works. Your role is to go to school and work hard to get the best grades you can possibly achieve. If you don't, you let yourself down. If any one of us does not put our best forward, we let ourselves down and the family doesn't work as well as it can and should. Do you get what I mean, Kristin?"

"Yes, Mom." My little body was shaking.

"If you really tried your hardest at school this time and a C was the best you could do in math, you should be proud of your grade. If not, you did not serve your role to the best of your ability." She reached over and placed her soft hand on top of mine.

I didn't feel good and now I knew why. It wasn't the C on my card; it was that I had a role and a job in the family and I hadn't done it well.

My mom kissed me on my forehead, wiped the tear just starting to fall, and said, "You'll do better next time. I know it."

As I sat on my couch with my glass of wine and feet on the coffee table, I knew exactly what I needed to do.

The problem is that I don't have a clue what success looks like in this situation, or how to achieve it. How can we develop a game plan, when I don't know the rules of the game? What does Oliver need from me so that we can win? I must figure out my role and contribution to this team and the company.

Over the next few days and weeks, I devoted myself to figuring out the marker of success and the game plan to make it happen, which included looking at our competition and the game they were playing.

Turns out our only competition was a similar newspaper tabloid technical publication. Now there were only two newspapers left that covered this technical market. Our competition had a similar sales team setup with a district sales manager and inside sales support, so it looked like an "apples to apples" comparison for customers from my perspective.

Quickly, I learned the competition wasn't going to make this easy, but not because the product was better. It was personal. The sales team we competed against didn't just talk business, they tried to undermine us with what I would soon call "trash talk." We were the "new guys" and had to prove ourselves—unlike the gentleman who sold advertising for our competition who was easy on the eyes, had been in the market for over a year, and had relationships established. People *loved* him.

So, we started working the territory. Oliver made sales calls, and I helped him prep and follow up.

People liked Oliver, but I soon learned that customers didn't want to change, or even try something new. Determined to succeed, I knew I had to do something to improve our chances of winning the accounts.

This is not going to be easy.

One day, Oliver asked me to visit a client with him. This time, walking up to the business building, I was more intrigued than anxious. I still had so much to learn, but I knew that seeing what Oliver did would help me help him.

We were meeting the founder of the company who greeted us in the lobby. He was a nice man, maybe about ten years older than us, with a stocky build and a hearty laugh. As we toured the building, I learned so much about the company we were visiting; but more importantly, I learned what Oliver had that no one could challenge— *intellectual respect.* I watched the founder talk with Oliver about a variety of technologies and markets and felt like they were speaking a different language. But I was fascinated by what else I was witnessing.

When Oliver spoke, this guy leaned in; when he asked a question, I could see both delight and dismay float across the gentleman's face. I could tell Oliver was asking questions that the founder had never considered and was obviously intrigued to be challenged to think differently.

This is it! This is how we are going to make this work—tapping into Oliver's intelligence, natural curiosity, and integrity to sell what he believes in and my ability to manage customer relationships. Now we have clear and distinct roles to make it work.

I got back to the office and started reorganizing our proposals to reflect a section "for consideration." This section allowed us to put ideas into the proposal that the company might want to consider; though it wasn't directly tied to the sale of our product, it showed we cared beyond making the sale.

We went from an "us against the world" mentality to winning business, and winning felt great! I was so excited every time Oliver told me we won a trial campaign or contract. It was such a great feeling to know that in my supportive role, I contributed to Oliver's and the company's success.

I was incredibly proud of how we worked as a team. Every day, I gave it my best effort, and I knew Oliver appreciated my work; but I didn't know how much until the day we reviewed our numbers.

The holidays were around the corner, and our business year was coming to a close. He and I were sitting in his office, realizing that we had not passed the competition in market share, but had made a very respectable showing these first six months.

His fingers were fidgeting as he praised me for my contributions to the success we were looking at on paper. "Kristin, I want to share this success with you. I want to give you this bonus." He leaned across the desk, handing me a folded piece of paper. "From me, not the company."

When I opened it, I gasped. It was a check for $500.

Mom was right. Not only do you feel proud when you do your best effort, it also gets rewarded.

The breeze was picking up just enough to cool the back of my neck that was now dripping with perspiration, relieving the urge to dive into the pool before finishing our conversation.

I looked over at her, noticing that at some point during the story, she had turned herself to face me as well.

I think her boss and president value her personal brand more than she does. I need to help her to understand what she gets and gives in this situation.

"As you can see, it makes a huge difference when you know how your role fits into the larger picture. Without this piece of the puzzle working effectively, it impacts the ability for others to perform successfully," I started.

"I guess I can. I suppose if they don't get the right people in place, they won't get the work completed that creates the growth." She adjusted her bikini for comfort.

"Exactly. I am glad you can see how your role fits in the larger picture. Now, I have a question for you. You said you came to the company to learn new things and develop, and that you did staffing before. What can you learn or expand and elevate by doing a similar role this time?" I held my hand up above my head to shade my eyes as I turned to look into her pretty blue ones, which showed me she was fully engaged.

"Well before, I worked at an agency where job openings were assigned to me—usually entry level positions. Now, I will be responsible for all job openings. So, I will learn about recruiting for all types of positions, technology, entry level, and marketing all the departments of a company."

I smiled as the possibilities emerged from her.

"And what can you elevate or contribute that might excite you?" I pushed.

"Well, now I will be responsible for onboarding employees. In my previous job at the agency, my responsibility ended when an offer was made, but now I get to help set the expectations and experience of all of our new team members." She sat up and faced me, eyes suddenly dancing with excitement.

"Your president and boss are probably counting on you to make that a positive experience."

"Yes, I think you might be right. Thanks, Aunt Kris!"

And with that, we both jumped into the deep end of the pool and enjoyed the rest of our afternoon chatting about life and eating some delicious chips and dip.

Less Than 1 Year Later...

"Aunt Kris, remember when we talked about me taking on recruiting at my company?" I had barely said "Hello" when she gushed her question.

"I do. Are you enjoying it?" It was a question I asked only to affirm the excitement I heard in her voice.

"Not only am I enjoying it, the president just gave me a spot bonus in recognition of how fast I have been able to contribute. They are also paying for my further development in certification courses. I couldn't wait to tell you!" she squealed.

I hung up the phone and placed it on the counter, just as the timer went off on the oven. It was time to enjoy my favorite lasagna.

CHAPTER THREE
DOOR NUMBER...

IT WAS EARLY Saturday morning and the heat was already beating down on the day. As I began tackling my long list of errands, I wondered how long it would be before I could settle back into my air-conditioned living room. The first task on my list was tending to banking details with my dad's estate.

Entering the bank, I headed to the podium where I signed in and waited. Not all the tellers or personal bankers were busy, and I expected to be called quickly. A few minutes passed, and I noticed that my impatience was rising to the surface as they continued their tasks, without glancing in my direction.

Why can't they just help me?

As I waited, I saw the caller ID pop up on my phone. It was one of my mentees who always texted me.

If he is calling me, this must be important.

I waved off the banker approaching me as I answered my phone.

"Aunt Kris, I have an opportunity at work, and I don't know what to do."

"Tell me all about it," I prompted and then sunk into the high-back chair to listen.

I always admired the calm, measured manner that was his natural communication style. Yet, as he continued to describe the situation, I heard the growing uncertainty in his voice. "I have been in my current department for almost ten years, and I informed my boss a while ago in a review that I had interest in exploring opportunities in the Investigation Department if an opportunity came up. Well, one recently did, and I want to apply for it."

This doesn't sound that difficult. Why is he perplexed?

"That sounds great. What's the issue?" I probed.

"Well, now in my current department, there is a promotion opportunity, and my boss has asked me to apply." He sounded absolutely exasperated.

Ah, now this is making sense. He likes it when things are straight-forward and logical.

"Oh my goodness, so now you have a couple choices. Sometimes, it's hard to decide. Reminds me of when I had to choose between two good positions…"

As I stood in the long line of people rolling suitcases, my nerves were getting the better of me. My throat was dry like desert sand, and I was shaking uncontrollably inside.

Why do I feel a need to look over my shoulder as if someone is following me?

Even though I was certain I wasn't doing anything wrong, I was fraught with worry that people would find out what I was doing before I had the chance to make up my mind.

Will taking a couple vacation days with only one day's notice send a red flag that something is up? I'm not really lying. When I asked for the time off, I said it was due to an unexpected last-minute opportunity to travel. No one needed to know the detail that it's to New York for a job interview, right?

I looked around the airport, hoping I wouldn't run into anyone I knew.

The security line started to move forward again, and I grasped my tote more tightly, thinking about the opportunity I'd been presented the week before.

Neil, the executive of our competition, had taken me to lunch and told me that he was looking for green talent with a lot of potential, and that my name had come up multiple times when he was asking around for leads. Flattered, I'd asked about the salary opportunity and nearly spit out my rigatoni when he said it could be double what I was making in my current job. All I needed to do was travel to New York for some quick interviews.

What will Oliver think of me if I decide to leave? He has given me a great opportunity, and this is how I pay him back? Although he is moving onto a new role in the company, if I left, the company would have to replace both of us. I mean—they wouldn't offer me his position, would they? That would be unheard of for a woman my age in this industry. I guess it's possible, but I've always been told that the way to move up the ladder quickly was to switch companies.

Loyalty is one of my biggest values—one I pride myself in. Oliver and the company had been so good to me. I felt as if I was betraying them by considering this opportunity.

You are here to get the facts, not make a decision, I coached myself, as I relaxed my grip on my suitcase.

As I handed my ticket to the young woman in her dark green uniform, I wondered if I was ready for the trip. The plan was for me to fly into JFK and go straight to the hotel. I was to meet Neil and the sales team (known in the industry as Neil's harem, as he had an all-female sales team) at Gotham about 8:00 p.m. for drinks.

Four hours later, I was sitting on a bar stool at tables of four, meeting the other team members who all shared stories about what it was like to work for Neil. I found myself getting excited, as if this were an exotic adventure.

I could be part of something really special.

That's when Neil pulled me aside. I looked up at him, noting his brightly colored Robert Graham dress shirt and black jeans. Struck by his confident demeanor, I knew at that moment that I wanted this job. He apparently wanted me to work for him, too, as he gave me the rundown of what to expect at the corporate offices the next day. Human Resources would give me an assessment test which he assured me was common, and not to worry. Then I would spend maybe five minutes in the president's office as a meet and greet.

Armed with that information, as soon as I could do so gracefully, I excused myself to go back to the hotel and prepare for the next day.

It was Fall in New York, and the air was crisp and colors changing. I was excited to wear my new pumpkin-colored wool suit from Ann Taylor. It was a stunning short skirt, fitted with a pumpkin-colored silk blouse and a matching wool jacket, accessorized with black patent leather stiletto heels and a matching bag.

With a three-hour time difference, I was worried about waking up early and having my "A" game; but when the alarm went off, I was already awake. My nerves were on accelerated mode, and I was rehearsing my day. I had given myself an extra hour than usual so I could take extra care in getting ready, but I lost track of time and panicked when saw the hotel clock with orange-yellow tone numbers display 6:55 a.m. Swearing at myself for being careless, as I had only five minutes to meet my car service, I quickly checked all the drawers to make sure I didn't leave anything behind.

That's when it happened.

Bending over to put on my heels, I didn't realize how close I was to the bureau drawer that I had left open. As I stood up, the corner of the drawer hit smack dab in the middle of my tailbone. Immediately, pain, like I had never experienced before, shot from the base of my spine to the top of my head. I felt like I was about to throw up, pass out, or both. I hobbled to the bathroom and raised my skirt. Peering at my back in the mirror, I spied a huge red welt about the size of a tennis ball.

With no time to feel sorry for myself, I grabbed my bags and a couple of tissues to dab away the tears threatening to burst forth. I hustled downstairs where I was told a car service would pick me up. I was stunned at what was waiting there.

This must be a mistake.

Waiting for me was a stretch limousine. My driver took my bags and smiled. I cautiously slid into the back seat. For the next forty-five minutes, I sat in the back of the limo, shifting from my right to my left butt cheek, as I could not sit square. And I prayed like I had never prayed before, just to survive the day.

The rest of the day was a whirlwind and not at all like Neil explained. For my HR assessment, I had to answer a series of questions. I sat in a small windowless room, with one hard folding style chair and a table. I was given a paper booklet that was a combination of fill in the blank and multiple-choice questions, and a final section where one was required to draw various things such as a house and a couple. This activity was meant to show some of my behavioral tendencies. I fretted about getting it right.

Do I draw people who are smiling or expressionless? How much detail does my house have? Windows, a yard with flowers, or shrubs or none? Is there a chimney and what about the style of the door? This is supposed to give the hiring professional insights into my subconscious?

Apparently, these behavior tests would tell them something about me as a salesperson. After the tests were done, I was asked to wait in a small office.

Lost in thought, I was startled when a young woman, in a smart black dress with her auburn hair in a bun at the nape of her neck, fluttered into the room. "I'm sorry. The president did not come into the office today. He's working from home. We hate to inconvenience you, but we have a driver to take you to his home where you two can meet." Normally I would be thrilled to have another ride in a plush limo, but with my tailbone still throbbing, I was dreading this trip.

My driver from the morning drove us about a half hour to Long Island. An older woman, dressed in a maid's uniform, answered the door when I arrived and pointed me to the backyard. When I reached it, Kurt, dressed in dark grey hiking pants and navy Henley, sporting Patagonia labels, was standing by a huge hole in the ground, which looked to be the beginning of swimming pool.

I soon realized that the five-minute meeting with this executive would not be as advertised. As we walked around the yard, and he explained the pool and concerns about what landscaping to put in, all I could think of was my shoes. I didn't weigh much, 115 soaking wet maybe, but the ground was so soft that my heels sank in with every step. So, I walked bearing all my weight on my toes, hoping to keep a steady stance, despite being distracted by the pain in my backside. Kurt stopped walking, and I snapped back to attention when he asked my thoughts about plants.

There was no interest in my qualifications, who I knew, or why I thought I should get this job. The voice in my head was screaming, *Where are the normal job interview questions?* With everything on the line, I tried to think of how to express my intelligence in the answer to the question. Trying hard to suppress the tone of "get me out of here," I reminded Kurt I was a native Californian and not an expert on varietals that would thrive on the East Coast. As I was participating and watching this conversation at the same time, I realized my mouth was still moving.

That inner voice said, *Focus, Kristin*, and I believe I suggested foliage that would not attract a lot of bees, as this would be a nuisance when entertaining.

He nodded and then ushered me inside where talked for another half hour, and then I was back in the limo on my way to JFK.

As I returned to California, I kept telling myself the situation was purely coincidental. I wasn't interviewing for another job because of what was happening at my publication, but I just felt I owed it to myself to explore this opportunity.

Why do I still feel so guilty?

Men were constantly moving around to further their careers; it just wasn't expected of women.

I felt paralyzed as I pondered what I would do if I was offered the job. I tried to calm myself by breathing deeply and purposefully, counting how many seconds it took me to exhale. When I reached nineteen seconds, I started to relax.

Why is making decisions so tough? How do I get "unstuck"?

As soon as I asked myself these questions, I found myself remembering a time when my mom had given me the answer.

Sitting in the kitchen with my mom as she prepped dinner, we watched *The Phil Donahue Show*. His voice sounded like a crooner with the excitement at times of an auctioneer. As I rocked in the recliner chair, I let my feet drag against the old fashion coiled rope wool rug while I listened to people share their most intimate problems on national TV.

These guests were talking about difficulty making critical life decisions—from leaving an abusive spouse, to what to do with an unplanned pregnancy, and other topics foreign to my thirteen-year-old world.

The more people talked about the problems they faced, the more "stuck" they seemed to be about what to do.

Is the fear of the unknown so paralyzing that they will stick with a known bad situation?

As I was thinking about this, my mom started to speak.

"Kristin, today is not what it was like in my day." She was shaking her head and stirring the pot at the same time.

"What do you mean, Mom?" I took the bait.

"No matter what choice you made, you were told, 'You've made your bed, now you have to lay in it.' Now today it seems there isn't any choice you make that you can't walk away from. If you don't like who you married, you get a divorce; and you can put a child up for adoption if you decide you don't want it. Now, I am not saying that if you are abused, you stick with it…but sometimes you do have to live through the tough times."

"Then, when do you know to make a change? How much time is enough time?" I asked, truly curious.

"Kristin, there isn't a hard and fast rule. You just know. All I am saying is that people get stuck because they think it's better to stay with the devil you know than the one you don't. That's the wrong way to look at making a choice. Ask yourself, 'What's the worst that can happen, and can I live with it?' Here's the secret: If you don't like that next decision, make another one. There's always another choice, so try a change; if it doesn't work, change again."

Suddenly, I had peace in my decision. Excited and nervous, I knew what I wanted to do. When they offered me the job, I thought, *What's the worst that can happen? If I fail miserably, I will just find another job. The potential reward more than outweighs the risk. Now I have to find a way to resign gracefully.*

I was sitting at my desk when Russ and a new executive from New York came into my office. Russ was not a typical executive. With white hair and a soothing fatherly voice, he was easy to talk to; and I was feeling relief that I did not have to leave Oliver, as he was already on his next move. Now with my decision made, it was Russ who would get the news.

As we exchanged pleasantries, I couldn't quite find the words. Finally, tripping over my thoughts, I interrupted him as he talked about what was next for the territory. "Russ, I have something I have to tell you. I got a job offer from the competition and I decided to take it."

The silence seemed to suck all the oxygen out of the room. When Russ asked what the job was, I mentioned I was given a district manager sales job. By the look on his face, I could tell he was stunned, but he quickly recovered, "Kristin, we don't think you're ready, but I wish you luck."

It didn't surprise me that my publication did not consider me for the district manager job to replace Oliver. In fact, it wasn't even part of the conversation. No one even suggested my name. But at the time, there weren't really a lot of women in that senior of a role in any of the publishing companies, mine or the competition.

Why would they consider me?

What surprised me was the casual tone of "wishing me luck."

I'd rather be good than lucky.

WOW, the bank is getting busy. How long have I been sitting here?

About half a dozen people were waiting to be called up for service by one of the bank employees. A teller motioned to me, and I held up two fingers, indicating that I would only be a moment more. She acknowledged me by nodding her head, and called the next person behind me.

I returned my attention to my mentee.

"Okay, so you have two opportunities. Well, you know your current department well, so let's talk about the opportunity in the Investigations Department first. Why were you interested in a transfer to that department?" I wanted to make sure he could see all of the facts.

"I have been doing my current job for so long that I feel I have learned what I can. I think I would learn a lot in the new department," he answered quickly and confidently.

"Well, that's important because you get to stay with your current employer, and it sounds like you can add skills and knowledge that may be transferrable to another job one day if you leave. Is this move to the Investigations Department at the same pay level as your current job? And what's the difference between the promotion in your current department?" I asked.

"I don't know." The uncertainty in his voice was back.

"Well, you need to find that out," I encouraged.

"I am afraid my boss who I really get along with will be upset if I don't take the promotion. How do I ask what the pay is without upsetting her?" he wondered out loud.

"From what you have told me, your boss has always been supportive of your career path at the company. Tell her how much you appreciate being considered for the promotion and remind her of your review discussion when you mentioned you might like to grow by having an opportunity on the Investigations team. Tell her you would like to research the two opportunities, so you can make the best decision for you and your career. Ask for help in getting the pay scale information and copies of the job duties."

"That's a great idea. I know my boss would like to help me," he agreed, his voice beginning to sound clear again.

"Then you have to weigh the facts on the pay. If the Investigations job is less, is that something you want to consider? Or because you have a growing family, maybe money is more important. If the pay is less with the new department, is the fact you will learn new skills and knowledge to prevent credit card fraud something that makes you more marketable if you ever leave your current employer?" I rapid-fired these questions, making sure that he looked at his whole life, not just his career.

"I see I have a lot of research and thinking to do, but my gut tells me I am ready for a new challenge and the promotion would not be as significant as a change."

"Good, you have some thoughts on your direction. Now you just need to get the facts and see if that supports your short- and long-term goals. Good luck, and let me know what you decide."

Two Years Later...

"Hey, Aunt Kris, I have to tell you something," he started the minute I picked up my phone.

"What's up?" I asked as I sat down on the couch.

"Remember I took that job in the Investigations Department?" he asked.

"Yes."

"Well, it's been a while now. I love what I am doing and I found out I am good at it. I have helped the department increase its successful fraud cases." His voice oozed pride.

"I am confused. What does successful fraud cases mean? I guess it's a good thing?" I wondered.

"Yes, it is. It means we are finding fraud earlier in the cycle and prosecuting successfully, which is a deterrent to others. I think I will move up in the department quickly."

"Wow, that sounds like a perfect fit for you. Thanks for the update—I'm glad to hear you're happy!"

We finished catching up on a few other things, and when we were done, I stood up to check on my pot of spaghetti.

CHAPTER FOUR
THE OPRAH EFFECT

IT WAS THE time of the year when the sun sets early and its changing colors, a rainbow of yellows and oranges, dance over the ocean. A spectacular view one should not miss.

Standing on the balcony of our host's home with a crisp rosé in hand, I waited for my mentee to join me. She had asked me to arrive an hour before our monthly women's meeting to talk about something that was bothering her. Feeling the cool breeze on my face, I relaxed into the scene of a momma grey whale and her calves gliding across the water and wondered if these majestic mammals experience the emotions of worry, doubt, joy, and love that human parents display toward their offspring. Completely mesmerized by the scene, I was startled for a moment when my mentee approached and started right in.

"Aunt Kris, they are making some changes at work, and I'm a little worried." Taking a sip of her cabernet, she looked at the sunset.

"What changes are they making?" I detected a bit of confusion.

I wish she arrived just ten minutes ago to see that momma whale and her calves. A sense of awe makes everything seem possible. We don't get caught up in our worry.

"Well, you know I have a marketing role in the company, right?" She turned her gaze back to me, and I noticed the fatigue around her pretty green eyes.

"Yes, you help with strategies for retail and grocery stores to get consumers to buy products, or something like that?"

"Yes, that's close. Well, now they want to change our compensation so that our bonuses are paid out based on the sales of the campaigns we launch. Honestly, I am not sure if I have the skills to do it. I can't control a lot of the variables and yet my pay is being tied to it."

"Well, what are the new skills you think you need, that you don't have?" I wanted her to see where she was getting stuck.

"I am not a salesperson. I don't close deals. I can't 'spin the truth.' Maybe I should look for another marketing job." She ran her hands through her shoulder-length brunette locks.

"Before you do that, let's talk about the possibility that you do have what it takes, and that this is just a little self-doubt that needs to be addressed. Trust me, I know exactly what it feels like to doubt my abilities…"

I was driving to Goleta to visit one of my advertising clients. Having just moved to a new publication in the company, I was glad this client was a fit for our audience, as I knew the two gentlemen running the company quite well. In fact, they had already given me a verbal agreement. With a 300-mile round trip ahead of me, at least I knew my time with the client would be productive.

Of course, a lot of my excitement was due to the fact that I was sitting in my new prized possession—a white 325i BMW with light tan interior. I didn't buy this car as a status symbol of my success, but because I loved the look of the tan interior with its small dot pattern and matching tan carpet. The driver's seat also hugged my small frame, and I felt a rush of power as soon as I sat behind the wheel.

Just beyond the Los Angeles traffic, I found myself on a two-lane road that hugged the coastline. I always loved the drive to Goleta, through Santa Barbara, arguably one of the state's most picturesque beaches. As I reveled in the beauty of the landscape, my thoughts went back to the childhood field trips to the Missions of California and the story of the Franciscans. Through the tinted window of my new sports car, I looked for the historical markers of El Camino Real, allowing myself to reminisce as I continued my drive.

Arriving at the restaurant early, I grabbed a table outside to enjoy the view, watch the surfers, and inhale the intoxicating smell of salted water until my clients arrived.

Over lunch and a little conversation, we executed the contract and said our goodbyes.

Back in my sweet ride and cruising down the highway, I was fiddling with the vents when I heard it. My heart skipped a beat. It happened so infrequently that I was always alarmed when it did.

I immediately pulled off the road and put my car into park.

Who could it be? I rarely give out my cell phone number. What's the emergency?

Digging my phone out from the bottom of my purse, I clicked it on and held it to my ear: "This is Kristin."

"Please hold for Mr. MacGinn."

My whole world started spinning.

Why would he want to speak with me? Breathe, Kristin. Breathe.

I felt sucker-punched as all the air left my body. I was shaking so hard that I could barely manage to hit the automatic window control to get some air.

"Hello, Kristin, it's nice to speak with you." The kind masculine voice of the founder of our company greeted me.

"Mr. MacGinn, the pleasure is mine. May I ask what I can do for you?"

How did he get my cell phone number? Why is he calling me? What could possibly compel one of the most successful entrepreneurs in the industry to call me on a Friday afternoon?

I tried to pull myself together and, noticing my death-grip on the steering wheel, quickly felt grateful this conversation was occurring on the phone.

"Kristin, I know you have served many roles in the company," he started.

"Yes, I started as a sales assistant years ago."

"I know, and it seems to me you have experienced many roles here," he continued.

"I have, and I appreciate the opportunities that have been given to me," I answered, wondering where this was going.

"Well, I would say they have been earned, not given. In any event, it's been a while since I have been in the field and interacted with customers. And since your current business unit is one of the newer ones, I thought it would be a good idea to get in the field."

"That makes sense," I nodded to myself.

Why is he telling me all this? What does this have to do with me?

"So, I have decided to see customers in the Bay Area next week, and I would like to spend half the day with your colleague and half the day visiting your customers with you."

Wait? What—what did he just say?

When I heard the words "next week," fear washed over me from head to toe.

Did I hear that right? Mr. MacGinn, the founder of the most successful technical publishing company, wants to travel with me next week, when I am going to be in Northern California seeing clients?

I knew I needed to respond, but the fear was choking me. Fortunately, some primal survival mode kicked in and I heard a voice that sounded like mine say, "Mr. MacGinn, it would be a pleasure to have you in my territory." That was my voice, my response—calm, controlled. My body and mind were not in agreement.

After hanging up, I sat in a pool of sweat on my tan leather seat before collecting myself enough to get back on the road. Instead of an enjoyable ride home after signing an annual contract, the drive turned into a long journey through profound self-doubt.

In congested traffic, with bumper-to-bumper red brake lights, I glanced at the time and suddenly remembered the digital clock from my childhood—and a promise I made to myself.

I looked over at the digital clock with its red, squared-angled numbers: 3:15 p.m.

Good, I am not too late for this episode of Oprah.

Dinner was already cooking in the crockpot, and the smell of beef stew permeated the air and made me dream of Pillsbury biscuits sprinkled with Parmesan cheese. With the meal under control, my mom was already sitting down.

This was a daily event—the two of us watching *Oprah*. It was the #1 rated show, and we never missed it. Her guest was a therapist talking about the "time out" chair.

Twenty minutes into the program, my mom started to shift in her wood glider with fall-colored cushions. The therapist was talking about the possible psychological harm done to children who have been spanked, explaining that a more appropriate measure is to give the child time to reflect on their behaviors until they agree to behave.

My mom became even more fidgety and began talking under her breath.

"Mom, what's the matter?" I asked, noticing that her lips were pursed as if she were about to cry.

"I never knew I was such a bad mother," she responded, with a tinge of sadness in her voice.

What? A bad mother? Why does she think that? I wondered to myself, not knowing what to say.

"Look over there, Kristin," she said, pointing at the wall with a paddle on it. The worn wood, the color of light maple syrup, still boasted a drawing of a mother deer and little doe and a poem that mentioned the paddle was for the "bottom" when the little one didn't behave. My mom hit our bottoms with that paddle, and my sister and I were grateful for it because it didn't sting nearly as much as her hand.

I sat there stunned, looking at my mom with her soft relaxed curls and her scrunched brow. How could she not know what a great mom she was? How could this "expert," who never met my mom, have caused her to feel so much self-doubt?

For the rest of that afternoon, she was more quiet than usual.

She shouldn't be upset. She's a good mom, I thought as I watched her doubts grow and her spirit shrink across the dinner table later that evening.

Because I knew the truth about my mom, it became obvious to me how destructive self-doubt could be if left unfettered.

I will never let self-doubt hold me back or shape my opinion of myself, I decided that night.

At fifteen years old, I had no idea how tough it would be to keep that promise once I hit the professional world.

This is it, Kristin, I coached myself as I took one last long glance in the mirror. *No self-doubt. You've got this!*

The day had arrived. Mr. MacGinn would travel with my counterpart in the morning, and I would meet them at noon and take him to my appointments for the rest of the day. Navigating the city would be more complicated than usual, as there were still many streets and bridges closed due to the big (1989) earthquake.

Mr. MacGinn, while a true American success story and self-made man, had the drivers and luxuries that his success afforded; I did not, and with no GPS for real-time data on closures and detours, I was worried about keeping us on schedule. Fortunately, Mr. MacGinn looked excited to assist me in navigation and quickly calmed my nerves. While his broad shoulders and impeccable suit exuded power, his soft eyes and sweet smile made me feel like I just got a big hug from my dad. Feeling a little better, I set us on the road to visit the top ad agencies of my clients, thinking about how eager they were to meet with us today.

Funny how people who always say "no" to appointments with me said "yes" because I have a "special guest" with me today.

As the day progressed, my confidence was restored, and relief was replacing any nervousness that remained. We headed to our last appointment, where we were meeting with the creative director of the biggest "get" in the ad industry. I had been working with the creative team and account management team at the agency for over six months, but we had hit a sticking point in getting the contract because the agency wanted access to our subscription list, which we didn't sell at the time.

While I can't blame the creative director for trying, it didn't make me happy when he asked Mr. MacGinn for access to the list not far into the meeting.

"Mr. MacGinn, it is nice to have you here at the agency. We love HCE and all its publications," the creative director started. I smiled at these two powerful men in their common world, yet the visuals were so different—MacGinn in a Brooks Brothers tailored suit and this creative director with a casual California look that screamed Berkeley.

"We appreciate the ad campaigns you have placed in our newspapers and magazines," MacGinn responded.

"When a campaign produces results, it makes sense." The creative director smiled wryly.

"Well, I am curious about something," Mr. MacGinn started.

"What is that?" the creative director asked.

"We started the publication Kristin represents about nine months ago. The demographics seem on target for at least three of your clients, so I am curious why you haven't placed any ad campaigns, or at least a trial campaign? That's why I am on this road trip, to hear directly from customers about what's holding them back."

"Oh, I see. Well, the circulation audit of the magazine does show that demographics of that magazine are a fit for several of our clients. It's just the product offering doesn't meet our strategy."

"Can you explain?" Mr. MacGinn probed. He tilted his head, to one side, obviously curious to hear the answer.

"We are working on developing a multichannel marketing approach for our clients—one that includes print ads, direct mail, and radio. Soon we plan to start advertising on the Internet. Your publication will not sell us mailing lists, so we cannot do a full campaign. That's why we haven't purchased a campaign."

"Well, that seems like an easy fix. You are saying if you can buy the mailing list, you would buy a campaign in this magazine?" MacGinn asked.

"Yes, that is what we are saying," the creative director affirmed, his smile suddenly looking like that of the Cheshire cat in Alice in Wonderland.

"Well then, let's do that," my boss nodded approvingly.

I was shocked when Mr. MacGinn said we could accommodate.

It required every ounce of self-control not to scream, "NO WAY!" but I just had to trust myself in the situation. I took a couple of deep breaths and reminded the creative director that it was the company's policy not to release our subscriber data on magazines less than two years old. I then addressed Mr. MacGinn, figuring this was a detail he hadn't been given, "When and if we do start to sell subscriber lists, we will work with the agency to launch and test the program, given their high level of interest. However, we invited the client to place ads in our publication to reach the audience."

With an approving nod and wide smile from Mr. MacGinn, I knew I was good at this game.

Self-doubt, no more.

The sun set quickly. The last sliver of the bright yellow orb appeared to be sinking into the Pacific Ocean. With the sky a light greyish blue, I knew that darkness would be upon us soon and the ladies would be arriving in a few minutes. I walked over to the beverage table to top off my wine glass and turned my attention back to my mentee.

"Didn't you tell me you currently make client and agency presentations?" I knew that self-doubt couldn't be overcome by me telling her that it was not well-founded. She needed to see that for herself.

"Yes." She nodded before taking another sip of wine.

"That's a form of selling—selling your ideas. What's going to be different about your job that they are making your bonus tied to sales performance?" I still couldn't figure out exactly what was the sticking point.

"Well, now I will have to visit retail locations and talk to store managers when we launch new campaigns." Her glass was almost empty, so she followed my lead and helped herself to more cabernet.

"Correct me if I'm wrong, but isn't that similar to the presentations you do today—but maybe tweaked a bit?" I asked gently.

"I am not sure I get what you mean?" Her furrowed brow told me she really didn't see where I was going.

"When you are presenting to the client or agency, you are selling your idea on the campaign features and how that will impact product sales, right?" I coaxed.

"Yeah, that's right."

"And I am guessing part of that discussion around what success looks like is talking about product placement, timing, signage, etc. Is that true?"

"I think I see where you are going here, but tell me more." She leaned back against the balcony and took another sip of her wine.

"All I am trying to say is that you shouldn't doubt your skills. Consider that you are simply going to use them in a different way. Have you ever had a situation where you have seen your concept in a store, and the moment you see it, you have an idea on how it could be even better? Maybe there's a better space to put the campaign items? Or maybe you send out two marketing pieces and one looks better? Does that ever happen?"

"Yes, it does." She smiled, obviously remembering a few moments of making a difference with her skills.

"So, if part of your job is to have these visits and conversations with the store staff, do you think you might make suggestions and adjustments that may give you a better sales result?"

"Of course." Now she was smiling.

"Then I think you just learned how to sell." I winked at her, and she laughed in response.

"Okay, I hear you."

A Little More Than a Year Later...

"Hi, Aunt Kris."

"Hi, so glad you could make it to the barbeque!" I gave her a quick hug, noticing that she looked so excited, like she was ready to jump out of her skin.

"I couldn't wait to see you. We just finished our first year with the new compensation and our bonuses tied to sales."

"Don't keep me waiting. Did you earn your full bonus?" I looked up from the barbecue to see her eyes dance.

"Oh my gosh, not only did I earn the full bonus, I was on the top team, and we get a one-week all expenses paid trip to the sales meeting in Hawaii. We leave next week!" She was quite literally bouncing up and down with excitement.

"Well, Aloha!" I gave her another quick hug and caught up for a few more minutes before she headed home to pack and I turned my attention back to the ribs on the barbecue.

CHAPTER FIVE
TOOTHPASTE DIVORCE

IT WAS A typical day at work, but the heavy traffic on the 5-freeway exhausted me. Not even a playlist of Motown's Greatest hits could energize me. As I walked through my front door, I had only ten or fifteen minutes left before the call.

Good, just enough time to start boiling water for the pasta.

I heard the Skype ringtone on my computer in the room next to me and looked down at the clock on my phone.

Oh, he's calling early. This question must be important.

As I sat down at the computer, and pressed the button to receive the video call, I thought, *I love this technology. It makes these conversations so much more personal.*

"Aunt Kris, I have a question for you." He looked relaxed with a sparkle in his blue eyes that matched the old t-shirt hugging his athletic frame.

"Hey, you look good! The work world must be serving you well. What's your question?" I leaned back in my soft leather home office chair.

As he sipped from his Big Gulp cup, I thought, *Oh, I wish I'd had the time to fix a cup of tea.*

"Well, you know I did that internship at the firm my final year in college, and then they hired me full-time."

"Yes, I remember. We were all so proud of you for being the only intern they hired." I smiled at the memory.

"Now that I have been there almost a year, I feel as if things are changing. When I was there as an intern, I found everyone was very friendly and helpful."

"What do you mean?" I probed a bit.

Suddenly, his eyes got more serious and focused. "You told me to set high standards for myself and set my own sales goals that would challenge me to exceed the company goals."

"Yes, I remember giving you that advice." I nodded.

"Well, we just finished our third quarter, and I have hit or exceeded the company goal all three times." He said it matter-of-factly with barely a smile.

"That's terrific! What's the problem?" I praised him, and I'm sure my brow was furrowed with concern at his expression, or lack of it.

"Well, the team is not as friendly or helpful. All I am doing is my job." He looked down and away from the computer.

"Let me ask you a question," I started, hoping to get to the real issue.

"Sure." He looked back up and straight at me.

"Your teammates—are they working hard?"

"I assume so," he nodded. "I mean, they are not making their numbers every quarter, but they are close; and some of them make or exceed it like me."

"When you joined the team, what were the other team members' numbers like?"

"The team was over quota when I joined, and I felt pressure to contribute. I was so stressed. Remember? That's when I came to you for advice." His shoulders were now up by his ears in an anxious shrug, but I was starting to get an idea of what he was up against.

"I bet I know exactly what's happening. Let me share a story with you to see if this is what's going on in your office…"

I was sitting in my high-back office chair, trying to make sense of it all. Taking a deep breath, I spun around 180° to face the windows of my office, laid my head back, and shut my eyes. My windows offered a great view of a gorgeous atrium on the bottom floor of the building, but I had too much on my mind to enjoy it.

I had just finished lunch at the building's restaurant, Bistango, with a girlfriend. The restaurant had limited light in certain areas where premiere art was featured and the portrait lights provided the ambiance of a calm environment, which was great, because our conversation immediately brought my stress to the surface.

It seemed like an innocent question: "How is the new job?" Her eyes were bright and interested when she looked up from her soup bowl and waited for my response.

I told her it wasn't so new anymore—that I had my first year under my belt and was wildly successful, but I wanted to prove to myself that it wasn't a fluke and that I could do it again. As we chatted over butternut squash soup, I described the pressure I was feeling at work and in my chest. I took spoonful after spoonful, hoping the warm thick texture would calm me down, but it didn't. I barely made it through the lunch without bursting into tears, and then hustled back to my office quietly so that I could close the door and figure out what to do.

This anxiety has to stop, I thought as I sat facing the window, trying to breathe through the pressure increasing in my chest. *I've never felt this before.*

I was used to pressure, mostly self-inflicted, but this was like nothing I'd ever faced. I worked on a great team, but I was starting to feel resentment from them and others in the office.

Is it my imagination?

I was consistent in my work ethic, and I treated clients with respect. I was friendly in an authentic way. The reward was continued business. It was that simple.

Why can't people realize that any success I have adds to the collective success of the sales team?

I had started to notice snide remarks on sales calls, where they belittled my accomplishments by calling me a "sandbagger"—a person in sales who holds sales and turns them in at the last possible moment to look like a hero.

Seriously, I don't have that much energy to keep track. And what if I forgot an order? Then the client's ad would miss the publication. "Book early, book often," that's my motto. And now my quota is significantly raised after I proved the market's potential, so I really have to put the pedal to the metal. What will they say when I surpass my current success?

I could hear colleagues bustling and talking outside my office door. One of the business units was up against a deadline, so there was a lot of frenetic energy. Every time a contract came over the fax machine, I heard a beep, followed by someone ringing the bell to signal that a sale was made, and then a group cheer. Publication deadlines were always a bit stressful, which is why I did my best to avoid the stress by hitting my sales goals before the deadline. At least I tried.

When did things change, and why didn't I realize it? Everything started out great. Everyone got along.

I shifted to a more comfortable position in my chair.

Why am I feeling guilty for consistent success, and why do others care so much about it? Is this the price of success?

Suddenly, my mom's words floated through my mind.

Could that be what is happening here?

My mother and I were having our usual late afternoon date, watching a top talk show program. I was eating a slice of banana nut bread just out of the oven, listening to someone talk about divorce. Divorce was still infrequent, but becoming more and more common, so many talk shows spent a lot of time covering the topic from different angles. My mom sat still in her chair, shaking her head so hard that her brown hair rustled against her light blue and pink floral cotton shirt.

"That's a toothpaste divorce," my mother said out loud, as if she were the only one in the room.

"What do you mean, Mom?" I asked.

"Honey, the problem today is that people stop dating." She said it so quickly and matter-of-factly that it caught me by surprise.

Stop dating? What? Is my mom advocating fooling around?

"Can you explain that a little more?" I asked.

She turned her head to look me straight in the eye while she made her point. "People fall in love and always put their best foot forward, and then they get up in front of all their family and friends and pledge lifelong love. But over time, they stop doing all the nice things they used to do when they were dating—all the little things that made the other one feel special and loved—and they grow apart. If you love someone, why wouldn't you continue to do all the nice things you did for them when you were single?" Her light hazel eyes gazed intensely at me as she asked that last question.

That makes a lot of sense. I nodded to her that I understood, and we turned our attention back to the show.

Maybe my colleagues fell out of love with the "new girl." They definitely are not doing the nice things. I'm going to have to talk to Daniella about this.

I waited for a "dating opportunity" with my boss, Daniella, to address what I was feeling. I lived in Orange County and travelled to the Bay Area so often that we had developed quite a friendship. Both of us loved to cook, and her stories of Italian family dinners in New York inspired my interest in Italian cooking. When she offered to have me over to her house to make the family "Sunday Gravy," a.k.a. red sauce, I knew it was the perfect time to talk to her about what was bothering me.

The natural light was abundant in her kitchen, as the San Francisco fog had disappeared. When she pulled the pot to make the gravy, I wondered if the pot was that huge or if her kitchen was just that small.

This is serious business.

As soon as we'd found our rhythm with the food prep, I started the conversation I'd been waiting to have. "Daniella, can I talk to you about something that is bothering me? I would like your advice."

"Sure, go head." She looked up at me long enough to shoot a smile before going back to chopping onions.

"The sales call last week…I was called out as a sandbagger. Do you think I am trying to sandbag business?"

"I wouldn't say I think you consistently are trying to sandbag, but it is true that you—maybe more than anyone on the team—have late sales posted just before the deadline."

"I know. It's just that I keep working it, and sometimes I get fortunate with late submissions. Either a campaign date is moved up or a new budget gets released," I began to explain.

"I know that can happen," she nodded. "I don't really see this as a problem and I don't think you should either." Her tone was just as matter-of-fact as my mom's had been that day in front of the television.

"Okay, it's just that when I started, I really felt embraced by the team. It was so exciting and I can never thank you and Neil enough for giving me a shot."

"Kristin, if you are going to be in this business, you need to know markets and sales territories have cycles. Sometimes everything is clicking, and sometimes not. What I am saying is that you will have your days when you feel the pressure because you are struggling to make the number, and others on the team are feeling that pressure at times as well. Their reaction is probably just a response to their pressure, and not a reflection on you."

"Thanks, Daniella. I appreciate you sharing your perspective." I took a deep breath and changed the subject to something lighter while we finished the meal.

On my drive back to the hotel, tummy bursting from an amazing Italian dinner, I thought back to the dating concept my mom shared and my business relationships.

With the backing of my boss and generally happy clients, I decided that I couldn't control others perceptions, so why try?

All I could control was my behavior. I would do the work as consistently and as well as when I started, and I would continue to do the "nice" thing in this business relationship and contribute to the team.

And I guess I could try new nice things to do.

I turned my attention back to my mentee and asked him to repeat the question, not sure I had heard all of it.

"So, you think people stopped dating at my work?" His eyes were wide with curiosity as he asked the question again.

"Yes, when people get a new job, there's something we call 'the honeymoon period.'" I could see by the way he cocked his head to the side he was not sure what I meant, so I explained further. "Everyone is on their best behavior; and over time, people don't keep up the standards they set in their honeymoon period. They stop doing all the nice things people typically do when they are trying to make a good impression."

"Are you saying that because I set my own high standards, that's the problem?" He was squinting now, trying to wrap his head around this possibility.

"When people hold themselves to higher standards than those placed on them, they continue to do the 'nice things,' which in your case means making the numbers consistently...so far."

"So far?" Now his eyes were big with alarm.

"If you decide to stay in sales, there will be many occasions when you do not hit your quota. You are new, and so you probably are working every piece of business out there."

"That's right! I am still stressed about making the numbers this quarter." He nodded, indicating that he was not free from the stress.

"Well, over time, you will find that there are conditions out of your control. Quotas not set correctly, customers' plans changing, new competition, disruptive new products or services…the list goes on. All you can control is your effort and actions."

"Okay, I get that." He nodded.

"Do you?" I pushed.

"Well, your tone tells me I am missing something," he said as he moved his fingers through his thick blonde hair.

"Most people, and you will too, get down on themselves when they are in sales and making the numbers seems difficult or, worse, unachievable. If you are consistently behaving according to your high standards, others may feel you are also holding *them* to those high standards. They may be feeling like they are not working hard enough when all you are doing are the 'nice things' like when you started."

"I think I know what you mean. I still make the minimum fifty prospecting calls a month, and I know some of the other team members do not. I don't think any of us like to prospect and hear 'no.'"

"That right. It's important to your management that you maintain that activity level, and that you do not 'stop,' even though it's not your favorite thing to do."

"So, what do I do?" he asked, still unsure.

"Nothing, except what you are already doing. You need to be considerate of your coworkers, and appreciate what stress they may be feeling; but my suggestion is to not worry about them. They will either learn to respect you or not. You can't control that. In your personal dating life, you want to be liked and that drives a lot of your behaviors, right?" I waited for him to nod before continuing, "In business, while you can learn from the analogy of dating, being liked should not drive your behavior as long as you are respectful of others."

"Thanks, Aunt Kris. That helps a lot." We chatted for a few minutes before the timer on my stove went off, letting me know the spaghetti was ready.

3 Months Later...

I answered the Skype ring on my computer.

"Hi, Aunt Kris." His expression was relaxed but not content.

"Hey, how did the last quarter end?" I asked as I cupped my hands around my mug of chamomile tea.

"Well, I missed my number by 6%. I am totally bummed out." I could sense his disappointment in himself as he hung his head low.

"What happened?"

"Well, it was announced that one of my clients is being acquired by the competition, and all buying was frozen." He shook his head in frustration.

"Ugh, hate it when that happens. What did you learn from this experience?" I inquired.

"Well, I guess what you told me about things being out of my control happening. I also learned how it feels when you know you have worked every possible piece of business and yet have come up short. I think I have more respect for some of my colleagues for when they struggle to make the number now."

"Understanding this dynamic in sales will serve you well. There's always next quarter. Keep me posted. Now, I need to go make dinner."

CHAPTER SIX
WHAT'S IN IT FOR ME?

WHEN THE SOUNDS echoed through the house, I wondered if my mentee had jumped out of her socks on the doorstep.

I hated this time of year. Every time that bell was pushed, the house was filled with spooky sounds of creatures howling, witches cackling, and ghosts screaming "Boo!" My husband loved to program the doorbell to the sounds of Halloween, but I hated putting my guests through that.

She will have to wait a minute. I must get the croissants out of the oven before they burn.

Croissants safe, I raced to the door. When I opened it, I smelled the berries before I saw the small basket she had brought to our continental breakfast buffet. I looked from the basket to the face of one of the smartest young professionals I had met. Dressed casually in Capri pants and her UCLA t-shirt, her long blonde hair was in a ponytail, and her normally clear, happy eyes were a little dark behind her fashionable brown reading glasses.

With jam and butter set on the kitchen table, I poured two cups of strong black coffee and smiled when she began talking before I even sat down.

"Aunt Kris, I am a bit ticked off about work and not sure what to do," she huffed as she reached for the creamer.

"What's the problem?" Spreading butter and jam on a bite size piece of croissant, I placed the pastry in my mouth and gave her my full attention. (Well, besides the attention I was giving to the freshly baked yumminess.)

"In my last review, we discussed career development, and I said I wanted to learn more and grow my role as an analyst. I finally am starting to get assigned to projects to build my knowledge in analytics, but my old duties are still on my plate. It doesn't seem fair. What should I do?"

"Oh yeah, I remember that feeling. This happened to me when I was offered a promotion that came with a lot of baggage..."

It was early Fall and the office had a window that overlooked the parking lot, offering sunlight tempered by clouds. I liked to take an early lunch and the growl in my tummy told me it was just about time to eat.

Maybe food will help, I thought as I lifted my oversized coffee mug and cupped it with both hands to warm them while I inhaled the strong brew. I hoped it would serve as therapy to clear my thoughts.

The Xerox machine was outside our office door, and its melodic sound was soothing. I knew I had to make a decision soon. It was the last month of our fiscal business year, and the machine was in hyper-drive, processing many sales contracts and proposals. Everyone was furiously trying to get all the business in the books and make or exceed quota.

I shut my eyes tightly and tried to calm my thoughts with the rhythm of the machine.

Management needed my decision so plans could be put in place before we started our new business year, but I was pissed off on many levels—the first one being that I was offered a promotion, veiled as a carrot, to get me to say "yes" to something that those who knew me would bet it all on me saying "no." In order to get that next level title, I would have to take on one of the least-liked and sometimes-combative executives as my collaborator to grow the business. Who would say "yes" to that?

Is it because I am a woman and promotions aren't offered based on merit? We have to take on additional "baggage" to get ahead—do more, get less, and be grateful?

Just months before, at a casual sales gathering, a senior executive, attempting to give me a compliment, had told everyone that I had more "cojones" than most of the men. I let it slide, as I knew it was not said with malicious tone and, on some level, it was true.

I took out a piece of paper and my gold and black Mont Blanc pen. Rolling the thick smooth chamber of the pen in my hand, I slowly drew a large "T" on the sheet. It was so easy for me to list the benefits to the company on the left of the "T," but I struggled to list benefits to me.

That's when it hit me—my mother's voice ringing in my ears...

It was a Saturday morning and a rare weekend that I was not at the beach apartment. My boyfriend of almost four years was out of town, so I had planned to spend the weekend in Anaheim with my mom. When I arrived, I found her drinking coffee and smoking a cigarette in the backyard. She was perched under a thin metal awning with spiral posts all painted white, overlooking three of the original orange trees for which our county was named.

We didn't have a lot growing up, but I had always felt secure and happy. Looking out over the yard brought back a lot of memories, my favorite being the summers when, in-between the orange trees, my dad and I planted a garden and I wore my favorite dress for the event. Properly dressed in a short sleeve blue dress with red dots and a white collar, I helped him push seeds in the wet dirt into mounds, so that when we watered, it would run down the canals. Then we watched and waited until little green plants started to sprout.

Smiling at the memory, I grabbed a cup of coffee, joined my mom, and watched her exhale a drag of her cigarette. Just sitting in her presence made me feel all the feelings I'd been ignoring for the last few weeks.

On the surface, I had it all—a great sales career that paid more than most college graduates could wish for, a boyfriend with a successful career that provided travel opportunities, and a beautiful place on the beach.

Why am I feeling so—ugh—I can't even put a word to it? I am just tired and uninterested. Is that it?

I gingerly raised the topic of how I was feeling with my mom. She glanced at me with her calm hazel eyes, assuring me of her confidence in my ability to figure this out on my own. Still, I was feeling like a child who carefully treads out to the Christmas tree to try to sneak a peek at Santa, with both anticipation and fear, and I soon figured out why.

The moment I started, it was like a dam had burst. After listening to me babble for what seemed an eternity, my mom spoke. There was no emotion. It was one factual statement graced with an all-knowing smile: "Kristin, marriage is never 50/50."

"What does that mean?" I asked.

She took another long drag before explaining, "Kristin, all relationships—marriage, friendships, and business—are sometimes 70/30, sometimes 60/40, or some other mix. They rarely, if ever, are 50/50. The key is that you are not always on the giving side. Sometimes you give 70 and get 30, and sometimes you get the 70 and give 30. What you want is a balance—that you feel you get what you need for what you give."

Her words hit me like a brick and helped me to navigate the feelings of imbalance I'd brought with me that day.

That's it.

With those words ringing through my mind, I knew what I needed to do. I was with the company when they changed their sales model. No longer were sales reps just geography-based; we were assigned to specific product groups, so we could build industry and product knowledge to benefit our customers.

During the first year, I was assigned to a product group that had mature leadership and was both sales savvy and friendly. I had built a solid business amongst my clients and benefited both financially and emotionally—I had high job satisfaction. I was getting the 70+% out of this relationship.

Now there was a need—a real need—and my management team felt I was one who could handle the job. If I said "yes" to taking on this assignment, I was going to be assigned to (fairly or unfairly) the product group that was viewed as the least sales friendly.

What do I need to get out of their 30-40% this year in order to feel good about this relationship? If I am going to give 60-70% to help this product group grow sales, I have to answer the WIIFM question: What is in it for me?

I created a list that I felt was a "fair ask":

- New title

- Pay increase

- Ability to show I could turn around a tough situation

- Build my brand through visibility with new stakeholders

- Be known as a "team player"

After gaining agreement to these terms, I accepted the challenge to build the sales practice in the new content area and kept that handwritten list handy for reference when I had exceptionally challenging days.

Topping off our two cups of coffee, I returned to the kitchen table where my mentee was quietly reflecting on what I'd just shared. I noticed the crumbs of buttery crust were scattered on the white table cloth and just a few berries left in the bowl with the silver serving spoon. We had truly enjoyed our continental breakfast.

"This is one of those moments where you have to assess your give and take. But first, I think it's important to acknowledge that the company is taking a step to build knowledge in an area where you expressed interest, right?" I put a little creamer in my coffee and stirred it in.

"Yes, that's right," she said as she took another sip of the steaming hot drink.

"Secondly, I think it's important to look at the give and take you've already experienced with them. Remember when you had only two classes left to finish your certification?" I sat back in my chair and wrapped my hands around the warm cup.

"Yes."

"What did your boss arrange for you?" Taking a sip, I waited for her to answer.

"I was allowed to have a modified, flexible schedule for six months so that I could take the classes when they were offered and not wait until the next session when evening classes opened up." She pressed her fingers against a few crumbs.

"Right. Do you see how in that situation, they gave a little more? I mean, wouldn't it have been easier to keep your schedule stable so there was little or no impact to the work?"

"Oh, I see what you are saying. So now it's my turn to do a little more and, on balance, it's closer to 50/50?" She dropped the crumbs from her fingertips onto the plate still sitting in front of her.

"That's right. And you need to recognize that not only are they asking you to do a little more, they are asking you to do something that will ultimately progress your career goals. So, it's a later payoff." I smiled, knowing that this girl was going to go far.

So much ambition in this one. I love it!

"Hey, Aunt Kris, I am not as ticked off anymore. Thanks!" she scrunched her nose and laughed at how easy that was.

"You're welcome. Just remember, the pendulum needs to swing both ways. It cannot get stuck on one side, so make sure the balance moves over time."

"I got it. Thanks, Aunt Kris." She took a sip of coffee and turned the conversation to her new love interest.

6 Months Later...

We were just beginning another delightful breakfast when she blurted, "Aunt Kris, reviews are coming up again soon, and I know am being considered for a full-time Level 1 Analyst position."

"Great news! Happy to hear things are working out, and you're seeing the balance."

"Yes! I love the balance!" she smiled. "Now, can I get one of those croissants?"

"Oh yeah, let's dig in."

CHAPTER SEVEN
SAYING NO TO A NUN

THE SMARTPHONE BEGAN vibrating and dancing across the smooth white desk.

Hmmm 3:45 p.m. meeting alert. Knowing her, she will be early. Best I let the front desk know to sign her in and send her to my office.

Moments later, my desk phone rang and confirmed the meeting with my mentee would start a few minutes early.

"So happy to see you today," I greeted her at the door, immediately noticing that despite her forced smile and perfectly-made-up face, something wasn't right. Her posture was usually confident, but at the moment her shoulders dipped forward and her eyes looked tired and worried. "Let's go to the break room and grab a couple of drinks."

"That sounds great. I appreciate you making time to meet on such short notice."

Wow, even her voice is riddled with stress!

"Aunt Kris, I have an issue at work I want to discuss with you," she said as soon as we reached the door of the break room.

"What is going on?" Knowing her well, there was no need to ask what she wanted to drink. Pulling two glasses from the cupboard, I motioned for her to make herself comfortable at one of the nearby tables and poured two unsweetened ice teas.

"Well, our company was sold last year, and the new management has put in new expectations of the client services team, specifically for people in management roles like mine." She had slumped into the chair, no longer trying to hide her feelings.

"How have the expectations changed?" Grabbing a bowl, I poured some peanut butter-filled pretzels for us and then sat across from her.

"The new director told us that he expects us to make sure the client experience is flawless, and that we need to work as many hours as it takes to keep the facility in shape to achieve that goal." She finished with a big sigh of frustration.

"Okay, so what's the problem? I mean, that probably means that if extra effort is required, you need to stay and make sure that gets done, right?" I probed.

"Sure, and don't get me wrong, I don't mind putting in extra effort when it's required. It's just…" her voice trailed off.

"Just what?" I pushed gently.

"Well, to achieve this, I am on the floor way too much, so I have to work a lot of extra hours to get my core job done. And it's the same for others…every day."

"So, what you are telling me is that in order to meet the expectations *and* do your core management duties, you have to stay extra hours every day?" I clarified.

"Yes." Her fatigue now showed in her eyes.

"How many hours, on average?" I asked.

"Everyone is working 10-12 hours every day." She frowned and took a sip of her iced tea.

"Ah, I see what you mean. That's not sustainable, and will cause burnout and turnover."

"Yes, people are getting really angry, and I feel like someone needs to tell the new director. Do you think I should say something?" Her voice wavered enough to tell me she was uncertain about the idea.

"Well, that depends…" I started, picking up a pretzel.

"On what?" She looked up from her glass to me.

"On whether or not you can weather the various consequences that may result from telling him. What do you think could happen?" I savored the pretzel while she answered.

"Well, my guess is one of two possibilities: He's either going to be happy to know, or unhappy with me for raising the issue and think I am troublemaker." She shook her head, revealing that she'd been stuck mulling over these options for too long.

"Ah yes, I remember a situation where I felt like I had to speak up for the people in my office. It was a tough one…"

The sales team had all been chatting via phone and email about the sales conference, and it was finally happening, but it wasn't off to a great start.

Everyone was asking who picked the place. Not only was it old and stank, it was dark and windowless. With only coffee, pitchers of ice water, and a small bowl of hard candy on the table, the planner obviously did not take into account that salespeople are a social, hungry, and somewhat picky bunch of personalities.

This is the environment they picked to start our sales year? Oh boy.

As our worldwide VP spoke, I stared down at my chair, noticing that its solid burgundy velvet cushion clashed with the floral carpet of green gold and red beneath it. I was trying to focus on his words, but being very sensitive to aromas, I started to feel nauseous from the smells of stale air, cigarette smoke, and air freshener. With the bile starting to rise in the back of my throat, I prayed I wouldn't throw up and distracted myself by tracing the small screw head on the side of my chair with my finger. The metal was cold, which I found soothing.

Feeling a little bit better, I looked back up at the VP and my surroundings.

The sales team was gathered from across the country, sitting at tables of ten, listening to our leader lay out the agenda. His tone was as cool as the metal on the chairs, as he recited the items we always discussed: new products, product changes, sales goals, and marketing campaigns to help us reach our goals.

I guess he's not going to discuss what we are all most curious about until later

We already knew there were going to be significant changes in the sales team, which is what he focused on for most of the opening session. The company wanted to organize customer accounts into three areas: 1) major accounts defined as multi-national businesses, 2) product likeness—group software accounts, hardware, etc. and 3) new business—companies who had yet to do business with us. The sales team would be assigned accounts and quotas based on these categories. Naturally, the most senior salespeople were assigned the major accounts that had products in many areas and did business all over the world. It was seen as a promotion to be responsible for an account like IBM, HP, or Microsoft.

I was grateful, not because I was assigned telecom accounts, but because I was able to stay on the same management team. I liked and respected my boss, so I felt less anxious about the pending compensation changes because who I worked for was equally important to me.

I've been at this for ten years and have experienced plenty of sales compensation changes. I just need to focus on which products pay the most and where I can find that business in my account base. This is not rocket science. I don't know what everyone is so worried about.

There was always whining when compensation changes were expected, as people don't like change, but this was more than the typical whining. There was a real concern for fairness, but I didn't know what we were looking at yet. I had learned it was best to work with facts rather than speculation in sales, so I was a bit more patient.

Well, I guess we'll see how this all rolls out, I thought as I grabbed my purse and headed to my room for the night.

The next morning, we met in our smaller teams and started to go over the sales plans, and that's when the first shocker came: The quotas—that looming number that you need to sell in order to make or break your earnings. As I heard the number in terms of a percentage of growth, even I had a hard time swallowing that increase.

Double-digit growth? In some cases, that's more than 50%!

The head of each product unit addressed the sales teams to talk about the product roadmap for their area, and the growth expectation was justified because it was the "Era of the Dot Com" boom.

I guess they're right. If the companies we called on are expecting ridiculous growth, so can we.

The night before the last day of meetings was our sales awards dinner. For what started off as a rough environment, they made it up that night with plenty of food and drink and music as people accepted a variety of awards for achievements. Like most award programs, it ended with a group of us in the bar enjoying drinks and talking.

I was sitting at the table with several of the people who were assigned major accounts. While their targets had grown, it wasn't at the rate of the smaller accounts. They were already getting multi-million-dollar contracts, so even a smaller percentage added up to a lot.

"The problem with the percentages is…" one of the heavy hitters started to explain why everyone had been murmuring.

Wait! What did she just say? I leaned in to make sure I heard every word. Suddenly, I understood why people were so concerned at the beginning of the week.

Many of our reps who had been with the company for a long time felt like the new sales reps, brought on to sell only new business, were getting a higher commission on every dollar they brought in. If they had to sell 10% more on a $7 million-dollar account, they felt they were paid less on that revenue than a new person with a $700,000 quota. Yet, it was the same amount of revenue growth to the company.

Now I get it. That isn't fair, I thought as I flung open the door to my hotel room a few hours later. *Someone has to say something!*

I was so angry, an intense sense of duty to say something growing in my chest. Anger mixed with alcohol, my body temperature felt like I had just come out of a day in the bright sun, only it was the dead of night. Thankfully, my room had windows that opened, so I let in some fresh air while I pondered what I should do…if anything. I could see the company's side of the argument, as well as the sales reps' side.

We were supposed to hear about the new compensation plan the next morning, and I had to wonder, *Does the vice president know he is going to have a possible mutiny on his hands? A revolt of seismic proportion?*

It didn't really impact me as much, but I couldn't shake the feeling that someone should let the vice president know what people were thinking. I didn't work directly with him that much, so I didn't need a strike against me.

Someone should say something. What would happen if I did?

As I laid on the bed and let the air cool me down, I was reminded what happened the first time I spoke up to authority.

I was playing in the backyard by myself. Against the fence was a playhouse, with a shingled roof and windows that opened, that I had filled with my dolls and toys. My best friend, Debbie, was out of town with her family, so I was playing house and tending to my dolls' every need—feeding, burping, and laying them down for a nap—when I heard my mom's voice.

"Kristin, we have some visitors. Please come in and join us."

Visitors? Wow! We hardly ever have visitors!

Usually, it was just the neighbors coming to have coffee with my mom and I was asked to "go play," not join.

I quickly laid my babies down to sleep and skipped with excitement to the sliding door at the back of the house where I entered the kitchen and immediately froze in my tracks.

It took less than a second for me to shift from excitement to complete fear. I always felt safe at home, like nothing could hurt me, but suddenly I was shaking and felt like I was about to cry. My mom was bringing a cake and coffee to the kitchen table where three nuns from our church sat on one side.

I didn't know why nuns scared me, but they did with their black or dark grey floor-length dresses with matching habits. In Sunday school, they were strict. You had to sit up straight, recite your prayers, and not talk unless asked. I never saw a nun hit anyone with a ruler, but all the kids talked about and feared it.

My thoughts stopped when my mom addressed me directly, "Kristin, with school starting in a few weeks, the sisters wanted to talk to me about changing your school. Since this decision impacts you, I thought you should listen to what they have to say." She patted the chair next to her and I sat down. My mom smiled to assure me it was going to be okay.

What? Change schools? I sat in silence and listened to their conversation. *But I don't want to change schools!*

I am not sure how long the conversation lasted, but it was long enough that I started fidgeting in my seat because I needed to go to the bathroom. Afraid that a decision would be made, I didn't dare move.

"Well, what do you think? Would you like to send your daughter to our school?" the older nun asked my mom. Her eyes were so dark that I wondered if everything she saw looked dark too.

My mom glanced at me, "Kristin, what do you think?"

Did she just ask me what I want?

She must have, because she repeated herself. "Kristin, what do you think? Do you want to go to St. Anthony's?" she prodded.

If I thought I was scared before, now I was terrified.

But she was persistent. "Kristin, I want to know what you want. If you had your choice, would you want to stay at Roosevelt or go to the school at St. Anthony's?"

"Mom, I want to stay at my school. I like it there, and all my friends are there." I'm sure my eyes were huge, and I could hear my voice shaking.

My mom smiled at me and turned back to our guests. "Thank you for coming by and inviting my daughter to St. Anthony's school, but Kristin has made her decision."

As soon as my mom started walking them to the front door, I ran down the hall to the bathroom.

When I came out, my mom gathered me into her arms and said, "I'm glad you told me what you wanted. I want you to be happy."

Starting to calm down on my hotel room bed, I wondered, *What might happen if I confront the vice president before the morning sales meeting, and let him know how people are feeling? I have nothing to gain and everything to lose, but I feel a responsibility to say something. I don't even know if he'll care to hear about it.*

Then the light bulb went on.

If I speak to the vice president, I need to answer the question of why he should care.

And that's exactly the approach I took the next morning when I saw him in the back of the conference room. Jim was dressed in a dark blazer, white shirt, and khaki pants—the casual executive's uniform we expected of a vice president.

"Jim, I was wondering if any of the discussion from the bar last night has been shared with you?" I smiled up at him.

"No, Kristin. I haven't heard anything. What's up?" He smiled back, genuinely curious.

"Well, after dinner, a lot of the sales people went to the bar, and many of the people assigned to our major accounts are very concerned with the fairness of the new sales compensation structure." I saw that he was ready to respond, so I took a beat.

"You know, Kristin, sales people always complain about sales comp changes. It's expected." Now he was fussing with the lapel mic, getting himself ready for the stage.

"I don't disagree with that. It's only…" my voice trailed off as I searched for the right words.

"Only what?" he asked, looking up from his mic and into my eyes.

"Well, a couple people mentioned they have been contacted by the competition to make a move. And seeing that these changes seem unfair to them, they may be more susceptible to the suggestion of changing companies. Didn't you say you put our 'A' players on these accounts?" I was determined to help him see the potential cost of him not paying attention to the grumbling.

"Yes, I did. They have a lot of tenure with our company and have relationships that reach wide and deep in these multi-national companies. It should have been seen as an honor and promotion to get an account like IBM." The frustration was beginning to bubble into his tone and onto his furrowed brow.

"Again, I don't disagree with that. I am just saying: What's the cost to replace one of these tenured reps if they were to leave? Time, money, disruption to the relationship of the account. It all costs money. I just thought you would want to know what they are talking about."

That got his attention.

"You're right. Even one sales person leaving would have a significant impact on our results this year. Did you get any idea what areas they thought were unfair?" He sat down and motioned for me to take the seat across the table from him.

Whew. I'm so glad he's going to listen to what the people are saying.

I sat down and shared what I had heard.

As we talked, it was obvious Jim was not willing to radically change the comp plan he spent months crafting and just announced. However, he did agree it would be a good idea to meet with the newly minted Major Accounts team and discuss their concerns.

Victory! At least a small one!

My mentee was still slumped in her chair. As I looked at her and sipped my iced tea, I remembered what I feared the most when I confronted management.

"Do you think he would fire you?" I asked.

"Fire me? Why?" She suddenly looked fearful.

"I don't know, but isn't that the worst possible outcome? What's your relationship like with him?" I probed.

"He always tells me I am doing a good job; and I have very high customer satisfaction scores, so that helps." She grabbed one of the pretzels and popped it in her mouth.

"Okay, here's what I suggest: Pick your *timing* and your *place*. Wait for the right opportunity or setting to raise the topic. You should also have this conversation in private, as you don't know what his reaction will be and privacy will reduce the possibility of him getting defensive."

"Okay, got it—timing, privacy. A good time would be after one of our morning business kick-off meetings," she said, confidence returning to her voice.

"What do you typically talk about in those meetings?" I asked.

"We go over guest counts for the day, and known issues with the facility, our quality metrics…"

"Hmmm, quality metrics, like the items you are doing on the floor each day?"

"Yes, that's right."

Aha! There it is!

"Here is something to think about. After a meeting where you have gone over the metrics and something is identified as an area for improvement, use it as an opportunity. I would ask him for a few minutes after the meeting to get clarification on an item discussed."

"Okay, then what?" She leaned forward, taking careful mental notes.

"Then approach just this area of improvement with a possible solution. While he may have already thought of it, ask if there is a business reason your team could not try it as a test for better outcomes. Now, of course, what you won't tell him is that your solution also leverages your team's time and priorities so all the work can get done in a reasonable amount of time."

"I can try that." She smiled at the approach.

"One more thing…"

"Yes?" Her eyes brightened.

"Try to gauge his receptiveness to hearing more. If he seems receptive, you may want to let him know employees are concerned with all the extra hours, and you are concerned morale may impact client experience or, worse, turnover."

"I see what you mean. I can try that." Now sitting upright, she looked ready for the challenge.

"Good luck! This is not easy, so let me know how it goes."

"I will," she said as she gave me a quick hug and grabbed a few pretzels for the road.

3 Months Later…

Packing up my leather briefcase at the end of a long day, I heard my phone ringing.

Oh, it's her! I wonder how things are going.

Still packing up, I answered on speakerphone.

"Hey, Aunt Kris! I finally had that conversation with my boss about hours."

"How did it go?" I asked.

"At first, he was surprised and a bit miffed that people were talking about too many hours. He said they should feel grateful to have a job. So maybe I shouldn't have shared too much. However, he did agree to let my team do a test and came around a little bit. I am hopeful it will continue to get better."

"That's all you can do. I'm glad you said something, and I bet he'll come around. Good luck!" I encouraged her.

"Thank you, Aunt Kris. I at least feel better taking some action."

As soon as we hung up, I snagged a single wrapped dark chocolate out of the bowl next to my desk and headed home.

CHAPTER EIGHT
CINNAMON CAKE

THE EVENING BREEZE made the backyard particularly peaceful, and the sound of the pool fountains lulled me into a tranquil state. It was the perfect way to let go of a long day. I glanced out at the patio from my kitchen, pleased with the simple presentation on the stone inlaid table, set with two stemless wine glasses and silver ice bucket. In the center was a small potted plant, bursting with light blue petit flowers.

As I turned my attention back to prepping a plate of cheese and crackers, I heard him enter through the front door.

I'm glad he feels comfortable walking right in. I smiled to myself.

I turned in time to see him looking as comfortable as he was behaving in an untucked, casual slate grey, soft cotton button down over jeans.

"Aunt Kris, I need some advice." His huge personality and smile matched his tall 6-foot frame.

"Sure thing. Grab this plate, and I'll carry the wine." I headed for the doorway leading to the patio. "What's up?"

"My main boss, the founder of the company, is out of town. And the next two executives called me into their office to discuss an upcoming change that I will have to tell my national team about. They said they are going to change the compensation during our sales year, and we are already half-way through the fiscal year." His tone was suddenly charged with frustration.

"That is a problem. Typically, compensation changes take place at the start of a new fiscal year. Did they give you a business reason for the timing of the change?" I reached for two of the glasses while he reached for the bottle.

"No, and there's more." The wine made a gurgling sound as he poured both glasses.

"In situations like this, there always is. Do tell." I grabbed my glass, and sat down before sipping it.

"Well, I went through everyone's forecasts against the new plan for the last half of this year. 100% of people will be making a minimum of 20% less if they hit 100% of quota, and management is insisting on making it retroactive." He was now unable to temper his anger.

"What! Retroactive? That's bullshit." I acknowledged that his feelings were absolutely valid.

"Yeah, that's what I thought. That means future commissions will be put against the overpayment of commissions for the first half of the year, and my people will be working for only salary the last half of the year." He looked at his glass and then took a good-sized swig.

"Wow. This is rough. So, what are you thinking?" I wanted to know how far he'd gotten into the problem-solving process.

"Well, I am closer to the president than these guys. Since he's out of town, I am not even sure he knows his executives are proposing this. I am going to speak to them again tomorrow and ask to speak to the president." His confidence faltered a bit.

"Well, I think that's the right thing to do. I am curious to see how that conversation goes. You know your integrity is a critical part of managing a sales team. Be careful and thoughtful about how you want to handle this."

"I will. This feels like a big test." He set the empty glass down and poured another.

"Trust me when I say that figuring out how to navigate this with your integrity intact is not going to be easy—but it will be worth it. I can say that with absolute certainty after an experience I had when I was in my early thirties like you…"

I wasn't looking for a job when Paola, my recruiter friend, called; but I had to take the interview. Her client was one of the largest computer companies in the world, and many would kill to have that name on their resume. Paola and I had worked together on a sales team in tech publishing; and while we weren't close friends, we were friendly, had mutual respect, and stayed in touch. She knew I had a few years in online advertising sales, which made me quite the expert in the industry.

Four days later, I found myself sitting at a hotel room desk, looking at a three-inch packed white binder, with no title sheet inside the clear plastic cover.

I was told to expect this, and I was feeling quite neutral about it. I had no butterflies in my stomach and no anger, even though I was expected to learn the contents of this full binder by 7:00 a.m. the next morning when my interviews (yes, that was plural) would begin. I slowly lifted the binder cover.

Here goes…

This was an amazing opportunity—the total sales package salary plus commission was $250K a year at target. The only downside was the commute to Los Angeles County from Orange County. A small price to pay for an opportunity like this.

The next morning, I walked into the HR office reception area, checked in, and sat down. The room was brightly painted with a yellow-orange shade of paint. On one wall, three very simple, but striking squared cylindrical flower vases hung from the ceiling by fishing line and showcased three Gerber daisies. It looked as though the flowers were floating on the wall, defying gravity.

That's how I feel now, I thought. I was mentally and physically present but not 100% there.

I couldn't stop thinking about what Paola had said when she first called with the opportunity: "The company is looking for a sales leader for its still emerging online sales team in Los Angeles. The compensation is at plan $250K, with a director level position. The team includes eight salespeople, and the current manager is staying on team. The company supported this person, but they just weren't right for the sales leadership role." My heart had raced with excitement until she said, "Kristin, this position has been open for six months."

Six months? What is wrong with this picture? Most people would kill to get this company on their resume! No matter what the personal cost, this is a game-changer in one's career. Could they not find good candidates? Were they too picky? Waiting to find someone who met 100%+ the qualities they were looking for? Is there something wrong with the team in Los Angeles?

"Kristin…"

Hearing my name brought me back to the HR lobby and kick-started a day that would include seven in-person interviews and end with a chat with the vice president to whom this position would report.

All seven of the people I met were directly assigned to the online advertising division, either in a sales or operations role. Things were moving quickly as I was passed from one person to another, like a side dish at the Thanksgiving table.

Over lunch, as I munched on a small salad of baby greens and sipped water, the salesperson and I had a thoughtful discussion. And just as in all my previous interviews, I couldn't stop wondering why this job had been open for six months.

As the day went on, I continued my fact-finding mission. Walking down long corridors with views to the outdoors, I saw how long this day had been. It had started with overcast skies, which turned sunny at lunchtime, and now the color outside was that of a fading sun. It was time to meet with the vice president; and having some idea of what was going on, I was really looking forward to this conversation.

I was escorted into his office. My sales experience had cultivated the habit of surveying a person's office to pick up clues on how to interact. His space oozed strength and power. He had a large mahogany desk that glimmered in the fading sunlight. On the right corner of his desk was a "boudoir-style" portrait of a woman. There were signed sports memorabilia, pictures of an athletic youth, and numerous framed awards on his power wall.

I quickly sized him up as I moved closer to the desk. Wearing a tailor designer navy suit, the man was not much taller than my 5' 6" frame, but his frame, sported with broad shoulders like a football player, spoke volumes of both strength and power.

"Kristin, it's nice to meet you. Please have a seat." He motioned to the chair sitting across from him. "Tell me about your day." He folded his hands in front of his chest and listened as I shared about the day, my findings, and some of the gaps I had already seen.

When I ended with, "It seems that the previous manager being left on the sales team might be an issue," I was stunned by his response.

He raised his voice and got argumentative with me. "That is not true. Who told you that? I want names." His tone told me there would be consequences.

Trying to appease him, I said, "Actually, no one told me anything directly. This is my opinion after a collection of discussions." He started to calm down, and I tried to change the subject by asking one of my standard questions: "What do you do to motivate and recognize your top performers?"

"I pat them on the ass, just like sports teams do in locker rooms!"

As the words finished tumbling out of his mouth, I sat dumbfounded. I couldn't respond. And I knew in an instant what I had to do: Get out!

"That's an interesting approach. Thank you so much for your time," I said, leaning forward to pick up my purse.

"Could you stay a bit longer? My boss is arriving later, and I think you should speak with him."

I hesitated but agreed and was quickly led to a lobby area with windows to the outside, where I could see the sky was now dark.

What in the world is going on with this company?

I shook my head and settled into a soft lobby chair. And suddenly, the answer came as I was transported to my childhood home.

I was walking home from school and looking forward to the first part of my afternoon routine: have a snack, do homework, and play if there is time before dinner.

When I walked into the house, I could tell today's treat was cinnamon cake. The aroma of sugar and cinnamon with a hint of butter wafted through the air. I was excited and rushed to the kitchen counter where it was always waiting for me, still warm, waiting to be cut into slices.

As I turned around the corner from the living room, I looked at the kitchen counter and saw it was empty. My mom was rushing around a bit, putting the mixing bowl in the sink with other dishes.

"Where's the cake?" I asked.

"It's still in the oven. My boss said I had to stay a little later on my shift and that made me late getting home." I noticed that she was still wearing her jeans and a plaid shirt, rather than her usual sweatpants and t-shirt.

She had recently taken a job at a local factory with one of the other moms in the neighborhood for the hours I was at school and we were both adjusting to the change.

I freaked out and started crying.

"Honey," she said as she sat down and invited me to sit on her lap. "I'm sorry the cake isn't done." She rubbed the small of my back to calm me down. When the sobbing subsided, she dried my tears and assured me, "The cake will be done in a couple of minutes."

Taking short gasps of breath, I found my words. "I'm not upset that the cake isn't finished. What if this happened again and you are so late that nobody is home when I come home from school? I will be alone."

She pulled me closer into a hug and held me until I stopped crying.

Within a week, my mom quit that job and told me, "Kristin, I thought I would work now that you are in school, and make some extra money. But I realized I don't like the extra money as much as I like being your full-time mom. I need to be who I am and you will learn one day to be who you are too."

While I waited in the lobby, his answer kept playing over in my head.

"How do I motivate people, you ask? I just like to give them a good pat on the ass."

Surely, he didn't just say that if I did a good job, he would pat my ass. Did he?

At 9:00 p.m., one of the assistants came out to explain there had been a delay, and I would not be meeting the executive this evening. "Can you meet with him tomorrow?"

"No, I can't. I have a conflict. I'll just have to reschedule," I said matter-of-factly, trying to hide my relief.

"I'll have our driver take you back to your hotel," she said, picking up the phone.

When I set my purse down on the hotel room desk, I looked at that three-ringed binder and shook my head. I was exhausted. My brain throbbed with pain, and my eyes felt dry and scratchy. I got myself ready for bed just in time for the inner war to begin.

Maybe I should still consider the job?

"You can't take the job! Did you hear what he said?"

I know, but I could do anything for a year, and that's all it would take to get a transfer internally and reap the benefits of having this company on my resume.

I stayed up all night, thinking and arguing with myself.

At the airport the next day, I called Paola and recounted the events from the day before. Even though I couldn't see her face, I knew she was about to spit out her drink when I gave her the answer to the motivation question. "I think this vice president, as well as the issues with leaving the previous manager on the team, are probably the reason the position has not been filled. I'm not going to pursue the opportunity. It isn't a matter if I can do the job; it comes down to the personal expense at which would I be doing it. I have the feeling that taking this job would require me to go against my values; and if I have learned anything from my career to this point, it is that all I have to take with me *is* my integrity."

"You know I respect you for that, Kristin," she said before we said our goodbyes.

Yeah, it's the only way that I can continue respecting myself.

The cheese plate was empty when he reached across the table to top off the wine glasses. A small hummingbird circled the night blooming jasmine plant—perpetual motion like the thoughts racing through my young mentee's head.

"It's not unusual to find ourselves in situations where we are being asked to compromise our feelings and our values. Our integrity is all we have at the end of the day." I smiled at him, knowing that he was a good guy and would do the right thing—whatever that was.

"I couldn't agree with you more. It will be interesting to see what the president says," and then he turned the conversation to the weekend's sports rivals.

2 Days Later...

I wonder what he meant in that text: He wants to see if I think he did something wrong? He is very impulsive, but has a good heart, so I doubt he has done anything wrong.

Sitting in my backyard with my laptop in front of me, I barely heard the phone ring over the calming sound of the pool fountains. Luckily, I picked up on the third ring.

"Hi, Aunt Kris. I wanted to check in after our discussion the other evening."

Dying with curiosity as to the meaning of his text, I wiped the condensation off the outside of my ice tea glass and took a quick sip before asking, "How did your conversation go with the president? Did he know what was going on?" I was a bit anxious.

"They wouldn't connect me to him, so we haven't spoken," he said flatly.

"So, what now? Just wait until he gets back?" I asked before I put a couple rosemary-roasted marcona almonds in my mouth. Left over from the night before, they were still delicious.

"They told me I have to inform my team of the changes. Then they asked me who I thought would be the first to quit, if anyone." I could hear his voice still tinged with contempt.

"And what did you say?" I took a bite of cheese with an almond, barely containing myself. I wanted to hear how he'd responded.

"'Me,' and I quit and walked out the door. I decided that if I couldn't get that support to speak to the president, I wasn't going to do this to my team. They would have to do it and own it."

I smiled. "That's a ballsy move. What do you think the president will say when he finds out?"

"I don't know. He's called my phone over half a dozen times, and I'm not ready to talk to him."

"Well, I'm proud of you for staying true to your own values. You haven't left anything behind that you can't get somewhere else in a heartbeat."

"Thanks, Aunt Kris."

CHAPTER NINE
YOU CAN HAVE IT ALL, BUT...

THIS CLOSE TO the ocean, the fog outside hid the sky's stars. The darkness outside made the kitchen lights seem brighter, and I saw my own image in the window, and my mentee approaching from behind.

This is ambitious even for you, Kristin. Making fortune cookies from scratch. Good thing she offered to come help.

She came straight from work, ready for another session with me, though still dressed in her grey wool pants and white linen top. I handed her an apron and wondered what was on her mind as I watched her struggle to tie the apron strings behind her back.

I bet that has more to do with why she wanted to see me than trying to tie a bow. Her petite 5' 4" frame and jet-black hair was packed with energy that was useful when she was a high school cheerleader and was helping her at the office. But right now, it looks to be creating some big frustration.

"Aunt Kris, can I ask you something?" she asked, still trying to tie the strings together.

"Sure, what's going on?" I motioned her to turn around and I tied the apron for her.

"You know Joe and I are getting married soon, and everyone keeps giving me so much advice that I am getting confused."

"What exactly is confusing you?" I handed her the bowl of dough and motioned for her to stir it.

"Well, you know there has been a bit of divorce in my family, and a lot of people are telling us that we should go to marriage counseling either at our church or with a family counselor. We have been together almost five years. Do you think we need to go to counseling? I mean, my friend did it when she got married two years ago and they just filed for a divorce." She looked up from her bowl to see my reaction.

"Well, I did not go to counseling when I was getting married, but I know a lot of people who did. It can be very useful. However, I don't know that counseling is what you should focus on, as much as a few key areas you two should discuss before marriage."

She finished mixing the cookie batter and handed me the bowl. "What are key areas?"

"Every couple is different; however, there are a few key areas that can cause friction for any couple, so you two should discuss those before you get married and make sure you are aligned. If you are, great; if not, try to find some compromise or agreement on how to work through these issues should they come up. As a very talented young professional, this is incredibly important. The clearer you are about who you are and what you want, the easier it will be to navigate the journey ahead with Joe. I count myself lucky that I had some clarity about 'having it all' before I got married…"

For months, I had been agonizing about losing what I had so desperately wanted (more importantly, needed) to fill out this great life in front of me.

Career—check!

Soul Mate—check!

Kids—hmmm, not yet!

Sitting in the office, I was anxious. My head felt too heavy for my neck to support it, and I wondered if everything people were saying was true. The gossip had been swirling around for weeks.

I wonder what the day will bring.

I could see everything and everyone moving around me, but I didn't feel present. It was like a movie was being made, and I was an extra waiting to be called for a scene.

I knew the market was changing, and not in a good way. Working in the technology industry for almost seven years, I had learned that the only constant was change. New technologies were introduced at what seemed the speed of light.

As someone who gets bored easily, I loved this fast-paced environment until our marketplace was really shrinking, disruptive technologies were on the rise, and those publications covering the new frontier captured the advertising dollars.

Why can't everything be going right at the same time? I finally have my love life in order, and now work starts falling apart. UGH.

I used to bounce into the office excited and curious about what the day would bring, but now it was stressful. I had a great working relationship with our clients, but now it felt strained. Advertising dollars were following the new publications. Clients had serious cases of FOMO (fear of missing out).

We were the new kids on the block once, and I knew the drill. Once one major advertiser said "yes" to try a new publication, the others quickly followed, all because of FOMO.

There were two publications left in my market space, and the rumors were that the market could only bear to support one of us.

I shut my eyes as the windows in my office started to shake and vibrate. *I hate those planes when they land.* Next to the airport, we constantly had noise from planes landing and taking off. *I wish I could get out of here now. I need to escape.*

I closed my eyes again and reflected on the last couple years—to the last time I escaped.

I had gotten out of a long-term relationship of almost five years. I left, and abruptly at that. It wasn't that he didn't care for me, or me for him. It just wasn't healthy, and I needed out. It wasn't kind or nice on my part, just necessary for my survival.

So, I buried myself in work, grateful it was there for me, while I travelled almost every week. I was done with men—well, relationships at least.

Alone and on my own, I did girls' weekends, accepted invitations for dates if I wanted, not thinking or wanting anything serious in terms of romance. I had been disappointed, and built a wall around my heart.

Single for over a year, I gave into my girlfriend's pressure to set me up. I didn't know why I had agreed, as I hated being set up and had no plans of settling down. She held a dinner party at her house and gathered our friends, and I agreed to make the meal and have just a "meet and greet" with a guy named Frank.

That night, lightning struck, only his name wasn't Frank. Unexpected. Unwanted. I had my career going at 100 MPH.

I could only see him from the back, but I could tell he was athletic. Not a football build but not lean like a baseball player. He was dressed for the beach in bright orange shorts and a sherbet green color cotton tank top. For me, the attraction was instant, primal, and intense.

What the hell is going on? My knees literally felt like they would give out.

I had just met the love of my life.

The women's movement had been promising for years—Career, Love, and Family too if you chose that for yourself. "Whatever you want, you can have it all!"

I don't know about that! I thought to myself as another plane rattled my office windows.

It felt like the other shoe was about to drop, or crash.

Is this divine intervention? Is the universe, in some perverse way, making my life decision for me?

The meeting on my calendar in the next hour would let me know.

With uncertainty for my job in the rumor mill, I tried to keep my focus on energy that was useful. I didn't know the facts, and until I did, focusing on speculation would do me no good. As hard as it was to focus, I thought about "having it all," and then memories of my mom and one of the most important bits of wisdom she ever shared with me rumbled into my mind as the planes continued to rumble overhead.

It was evening and the news was on in the background, on the little black and white TV in the corner of our kitchen. I was sitting on one of the wood barstools at the counter, so I could watch both the TV and my mom while she made dinner. That night, it was pork chops, and I couldn't wait to drown my plate in gravy.

The handsome broadcaster was talking about an event in LA that was part of the women's movement, and he addressed the reporter on the scene where the crowds were pushing for a position to get a glimpse of the interviewee—feminist activist, Jane Snow.

Even though I was only fifteen, I knew about this movement. Not because my mom was interested in it, but because my oldest sister had a career, marriage, and child. She had it *all*. She was the first generation of women who activists messaged about sexual liberation, equality, and "having it all."

The reporter asked: "Why do women have to choose between marriage, career, and family?"

Jane Snow answered quickly and confidently: "That's the beauty of the movement. Women don't have to choose. Now you can have a career, spouse, family, or any combination you want. You are the architect of your life. Now you *can* have it all!"

My mom's voice startled me: "That's a lot of baloney!"

Whoa! What's up with that, Mom? I looked at her closely, taking in her obvious dissatisfaction with the statement. Her lips were pursed and her dark hazel eyebrows scrunched together.

"Mom, what do you mean?"

"Kristin, I just get miffed when people get on TV and espouse a view for everyone." She shook her head disapprovingly as she opened the oven to check on the meal.

"Well, don't you think women should have all of these opportunities?" I asked.

"Yes, of course I do. Women should be able to do what they want. I mean, I grew up in the Depression Era and choices were limited. You were expected to get married and have a family, and that might not be right for everyone."

"Okay, so why the strong reaction to what Jane Snow said—that women have choices and can have it all?"

"Because it's only partly true." She put her towel down and walked over to me, to look me straight in the eyes.

"Which part?" I asked.

"Kristin, what people should realize is that yes, you can have it all—career, marriage, family—just not at the same time."

"Not at the same time?" I know my eyes were as big as my fifteen-year-old face.

"Yes, it is not reasonable to think you can work a big power job at 8+ hours a day, come home to a family that has needs, and have your full energy and effort for those needs. Something needs to give. And when it does, it's usually your own needs not being met. Who wins in that situation?"

"I guess I see your point." I nodded.

"It's about choices and timing. Once you know what you really want, go for it. If that's a career, go for that; if it's marriage and family, create that. Just don't try everything at once. I guess it gets my dander up when people try to say it can be done. You can have it all, Kristin, just not all at the same time…if you want the best outcome."

As we assembled in the conference room, our publisher made himself known on the conference line with a company-wide announcement: "The competition is buying us, and our jobs are being eliminated."

This is a first in my career—my first layoff.

The love of my life, who I'd met at the dinner party a year earlier, was on his way to the Midwest for graduate work. I no longer had to decide between my job and love. My job was no longer. We never talked about what would happen when he left, and now the opportunity was right in front of me.

Would I choose love?

Will he choose me?

The sweet smell of almond from the extract in the cookie batter enveloped the kitchen. When the timer started to beep, she went to the oven to remove the cookie sheets.

"That's why my recommendation is that you address these key areas of 'having it all' before you get married," I continued.

"What do you think these key areas are?" she asked as she handed me the spatula.

We had a plate of cookie do-overs—ones that cooled too quickly before we placed a fortune inside, wrapped in the traditional crescent shape—and I took a bite of one.

Mmmm…not bad. I handed her one of the misfit cookies to snack on.

"Well they may be different for each couple, but I can think of three that are the cause of a lot of disagreements or arguments: 1) money or how you use debt, 2) how you feel about children, and 3) if you are sexually compatible."

"I think we are pretty aligned in those areas."

"Are you?" I pushed gently, knowing she could take the challenge.

"You don't sound so sure?" she smiled curiously back at me.

"Well, let's take money and debt. You have a high-pressure job and you are rewarded through salary and bonus for your accomplishments, right?" I asked.

"I do make more than Joe by quite a bit," she confirmed.

"Correct, because you both picked career paths that make both of you happy professionally. However, over time, that earning disparity may cause friction. I mean, you do like to spend money and Joe seems to be more of a saver. Am I right?"

She nodded.

"All I am saying is talk about it. Talk about how much short-term versus long-term debt you both are comfortable with. Think of it as credit card balances versus debt for a mortgage." I decided to tackle the next big issue. "Now let's talk about how money may impact your decision around having a family. Do both you and Joe want a family?"

"Well, we don't want kids right away. We want to travel first, but yes, we have talked about it and we definitely want kids. Two, maybe three."

"Well, that's good you are aligned. May I challenge you a bit?"

"Sure, why not." She smiled again and continued moving the cookies from the sheet to the plate.

"What about when you have kids? Have you talked about child care? Or do you want to stop working and stay at home?"

"I definitely want to keep working. Since Joe is a teacher, we will only need day care during the school year, and he will be at home during summers. Once the kids are in school, they will all be on the same schedule. I think we are set on that plan."

"Are you really? Have you considered what happens when you have that first child? You don't know how you will feel once that little bundle of joy arrives. What if your feelings are so strong and you don't want to go back to work? Maybe not forever, but maybe the first year or longer. You don't know how you will feel until that child enters the world."

"I guess I see what you mean, but I am pretty sure I want to work after kids."

"That's great, but it would be good to keep the option open. See how this relates to the agreement on money? If you live where you have a mortgage that is not at your max and save, then when you start a family, *if* you decide you want to be home, you have that choice. Otherwise, you and Joe are putting pressure and resentment on your relationship or at least risk that."

"I guess I hear what you are saying."

"Let me leave you with this final thought. It's really difficult to have everything at once. You work a long day and then may be tired when you get home and not have the full energy you may want to have for your husband and kids. There is no wrong answer. Just talk about it and work through it so you and Joe are working as a team."

"Yes, I can do that. Thanks, Aunt Kris."

And with that, we went back to finishing the three dozen fortune cookies for the her and Joe's engagement party favors.

I Year Later...

Looking at my mentee struggling to slip swim floaties on her baby daughter's arms, I thought, *She is beaming with the pride of a new mother.*

"Hi, Aunt Kris. We appreciate your offer to come for a swim." She turned her smile toward me.

"Mommy and me classes are a great way to get back in shape and spend time with your baby, aren't they?" I smiled back and said hi to the beautiful baby girl with huge blue eyes like her momma.

"Aunt Kris, I just wanted to say thank you. Once Sonia was born, I did have mixed feelings about going back to work. Since you told me to have options, we did that; and so as hard as it was to return to work, it was what I wanted and not what I had to do for money."

"I am glad it worked out." I reached out for the baby, who was more interested in grabbing a cookie from the plate next to me when she held out her hands to me, and pulled her out of her mom's arms and walked into the water.

"It did. I mean, I won't say it wasn't hard going back to work. But at least it was my choice. I had the option to stay home or go back to work."

I slipped a crumb of cookie into the baby's mouth and smiled back at her mommy. "Well, it looks like this little one is super happy. And that's not just because of the tiny bit of cookie I just sneaked her."

CHAPTER TEN
THE GREATEST GENERATION

WALKING BACK INTO the house with a basket of clothes from the dryer, I saw him pulling into the driveway. He had sent a text late the night before, which I didn't answer until that morning. I was rather curious as to why he wanted to meet so quickly.

"Hi, Aunt Kris. Thanks for agreeing to meet me this weekend," the young man said as he stepped through my front door. Dressed in his Seahawks Jersey, obviously ready to hit the sports bar later that day to watch football with friends, his casual dress did not detract from his confident presence.

"My pleasure. I'm just doing stuff around the house. You said you had something to discuss? Is everything going okay with the new job?" I asked.

"I love the job. However, I have some concerns." He glanced around the room, one hand on the chair, unsure of whether to stand or sit down.

I set the laundry basket on the counter. He definitely wanted my attention.

I can fold and hang these later.

"How can I help?" I motioned for him to take a seat at the table, and grabbed the coffee to pour some for both of us.

"Well, it's just that I have been asked to go on a business trip with team members from various departments in a couple weeks. We have in-market events we are conducting." I placed the cup in front of him, and then grabbed a few biscotti cookies from the glass jar on the counter before joining him.

"Well, that sounds like fun. When I spent time on the road on team business trips, it allowed me to have experiences that forged better business relationships.'

"Yes, but…" he started.

"Yes, but…what?" I raised my eyebrow, wondering what could be worrying him.

"Yes, but I am concerned because I have heard stories of a few others on the trip. Let's just say we don't share the same ethic. I am concerned being new that their reputation may be assigned to me as well." He grabbed a biscotti and manhandled the delicate cookie.

Boy, he is stressed about this.

"How so?" I coaxed.

"Well, a couple of us are real foodies, and I picked out a restaurant I really want to go to because the chef is known for his molecular gastronomy. He is cutting-edge. I suggested one night we go to the restaurant." He smiled at me, acknowledging that this was a favorite pastime we had in common.

"Okay, so where's the catch?" I wondered.

"Well, everyone now wants to go, and I know for a fact they have abused their expense accounts; and I don't want to be associated with that. How can I avoid that?" he asked point blank.

"You have to decide if the price is worth taking a stand. I've learned, in twenty plus years of my career, that character and reputation are incredibly important…"

There were only twenty-six days before October 1, but this year it seemed to be approaching at lightning speed. It was the start of our new fiscal year and decisions had to be made quickly.

I hope we can just do what is right.

I had been apprehensive about this particular meeting, and not because I had to present to the senior leadership team. In my career, I'd often presented to senior leaders without much thought. But today, I could feel the blood pulsing through my veins and my jaw locked.

I have spent the last year doing what was asked of me. Will they accept my recommendation today?

It was five minutes to 10:00 a.m., and they would be entering the room at any minute. In the large conference room, everything was ready to go. My presentation was successfully projected onto the big screen that dropped down from the ceiling for occasions like this, covering the heavy mahogany bookcases. My handouts of detailed reports were ready to be handed out, should they want more data. Facilities had set up coffee and water service.

Everything is ready but me. My stomach was rolling, my throat was dry, and I felt stuck to my chair. I got up and poured myself a glass of water, trying to dispel the fear; but the tension continued to grow as I remembered what had brought me to this moment.

A year earlier, I was at home on a Saturday, sitting on the edge of the pool and chatting with my friends. While deep in conversation, I enjoyed the contrast of the hot sun on my face and the cool pool water on my legs. It was a typical warm California summer day, and I relished the aroma of meats and vegetables on our grill.

Getting up to check the food, I heard my phone ring and glanced at the caller ID. It was my boss.

Why is he calling me on the weekend?

I excused myself as I picked up the phone. "Hello, Justin. What do you need?"

"Kristin, remember when we talked about taking on a different assignment when the fiscal year starts?" he started.

"Yes, we talked about maybe needing help on building a team for Pascal's business unit to support clients who have business locations outside the U.S." I held the phone with one hand and opened the top of the barbecue with the other.

"Well, Pascal called and he definitely wants you on the team. He thinks you have the relationships with your colleagues, both inside the U.S. and outside in Europe and Asia, to help coordinate teams and reduce the tensions that we experienced this year." Justin's voice was hurried, but full of pride. We really had made a good team, and I could tell he was excited to see me get this opportunity.

"That sounds great. So why the call this weekend? Not that I mind you calling on a weekend, but what's the urgency? The new fiscal year is months away." I flipped the chicken legs over but stayed focused on the voice on the other side of the phone.

"Pascal is holding a team-building event in about ten days and he wants you to attend, so I wanted to let you know we need you to leave soon for Asia. Is that a problem?" he asked.

"No problem at all," I smiled. "I'll be there."

I got off the phone thrilled about the opportunity.

As a company, we wanted to take a "customer first" focus. We had learned that our large multi-national technology clients often were buying the same report or research in different country offices when the main U.S. headquarters location had already purchased it. In short, these companies needed help coordinating their purchases so they could save money, which we expected would be used to buy more from us.

I was asked to create and lead a team that would be the "go-to" internal resource for our U.S. and international sales organization. Whenever one of these multinational companies wanted to buy an out of market report, we would help coordinate and leverage any previous purchases. We were looking for *win-win* situations, and the team-building event was the start of that adventure. I hired two sales reps, and we focused on the regions of Asia Pacific and EEMEA (Eastern Europe, Middle East, and Africa) for coordinating client purchases.

Taking another gulp of the water, I sat back down in the leather chair at the end of the long, mahogany conference table.

Hard to believe that was a whole year ago! And now, I get to present the findings of our experiment and ask the leadership to make sure my team is well taken care of.

The familiar sight of one man's power suit after another entered the room. Variations of the same color palate with only one wearing this season's proclaimed power tie color—pale yellow. That was the senior vice president of sales. As they entered the room, I greeted them and stood to begin the presentation.

It's show time.

We had been trying to prove a hypothesis, and we gave it a year to prove it. To our surprise, the data did not suggest that the resources invested yielded a suitable return on investment.

My recommendation was to disband my team, and my "ask" was simple. We had two proven, trained sales reps who were suitable for positions opening at the start of the fiscal year—only weeks away. All I asked for was that we let the hiring manager and my team members know that they would be moving on to a new position next fiscal year.

When the meeting in the conference room ended, their answer was "no." Not only did they say "no," there was no appetite to revisit the issue.

"Kristin, if we were to announce that change now, it would cause a political problem with the markets vying for ownership. They will see it as a failure."

That meant that by the time my team members learned of the news, any openings for the new fiscal year would have been filled with new talent who needed to be trained. My two vested team members would be out of work—corporate collateral damage.

WTF?

I had never been so pissed off in all my life. My blood boiled so hard that I thought steam would release from my body, the way it does when a teakettle whistles.

What am I going to do? And suddenly, I remembered that my mom had already given me this answer.

Dressed in a familiar light floral shift over her clothes, her hair tightly-curled and teased from her weekly Saturday shampoo, Mom was preparing Sunday dinner, which was always fried chicken, mashed potatoes with homemade gravy, two vegetables, and red Jell-O. The only variation was whether there would be walnuts and thinly sliced bananas placed on top of the Jell-O.

I sat on a barstool at the counter and watched as she dropped the pieces of chicken into the oil of the well-worn avocado green electric fryer. It was the second batch, so the house was already filled with the aroma of grease and cooked flour and a seasoning that made the glands on the side of my jaw pucker. From where I sat, I could see all the brown bits from the frying in the pan—the secret to my mom's gravy.

Glancing away from the pan, I spotted a book on the table. It only stood out because it was a new book that everyone was talking about. My mother, always a voracious reader, was equally known for never buying a book new.

"Mom, is that a new book?"

Looking up from her pan to smile at me, she answered, "Yes, it's the one by Tom Brokaw, *The Greatest Generation*."

"I didn't think the library had it yet." I reached for the book and started flipping through it.

"They didn't. You know I don't like to spend money on books to read it once, but I made an exception, Kristin, because this is my generation. I was a young woman when our men went to fight in the war. Only a year older than you are now."

"Have you read it yet?" I asked, as I put the book down to pick at a piece of chicken and lick my fingers of the residue of salt and grease.

"I just finished it." She raised an eyebrow in my direction.

"What did you think?" I questioned.

"Well, Kristin, the men who came back from fighting in the war never talked about what happened there, including my brothers. Everyone did something for the war effort. Women went to work in factories because there weren't enough men."

"Do you think it was the greatest generation?" Now I raised my eyebrow.

"I don't know, but it's different from today, that's for sure." She nodded as she turned the chicken in the pan.

"What do you mean?" I snagged another bit of chicken and leaned forward on the counter.

"Everyone today is all about 'me, me, me.' People are trying to get ahead and make a name for themselves, but at what cost? We hear people getting reputations like 'greedy, gold digger and pushover' because they put themselves ahead of others or not. That's what was different about this generation."

"Oh, I get it, because they put others first. That's what made them great?" I cleaned my fingers and continued flipping through the book.

"No, not exactly. This generation had character, which is largely missing today. They lied about their age in some cases to get into the war early." She left the fryer for a moment to give the mashed potatoes some attention.

"Mom, you mentioned people making a name for themselves and their reputations, but this generation had character. I am not sure I understand the difference?" I knew she was making a point, but I couldn't quite grasp it.

"Kristin, character is made by what you stand for, reputation is made by what you fall for. If you stand for nothing, you will fall for anything. You have to be willing to put your integrity on the line and stand for something you believe in. Even at your own peril."

I know what I have to do.

As the leadership team stood to leave, I called out the senior vice president's name to stop him, which meant no one was leaving.

"Dan, are you sure you will not reconsider having my two members reassigned before the end of the fiscal year? We don't have to let everyone in on *why* this is happening so that it doesn't cause a problem."

"Kristin, I thought we made it abundantly clear. We are not releasing your recommendation until after the fiscal year plan is approved and broadly communicated." His tone was firm and a little annoyed.

"You did. It's just unfortunate. I enjoy working here." I leaned forward on the conference table for a little support.

"Well, nothing will change for you. We assured you we have a place for you next fiscal." He smiled reassuringly.

"While I appreciate that gesture, I'm resigning. I will have a formal letter on your desk by the end of the day." I picked up my things and left the room, noticing that all of the tension had left my body.

Yes, that was the right thing to do.

Sipping the still-hot coffee, I brought the conversation back to him. "You have to decide if the price is worth taking the stand."

He took a last sip of his coffee and grabbed a biscotti for the road. I noticed some optimism in his expression as he rose from his chair. "Thanks, Aunt Kris. You've given me a lot to think about." With a respectful nod, he walked toward the front door.

I laughed out loud as the door closed. *Well, seems he got what he needed. Time to get back to the laundry,* I thought as I finished the last bite of my biscotti.

Two Weeks Later...

When my mentee called during the week, asking if he could pop by on Football Sunday, of course I invited him over.

Thankfully, with the laundry finished, I could focus on him when he arrived. *Wow, his walk is a lot more relaxed. That is a good sign.*

Excitedly, he started talking before he was all the way in the house, "Aunt Kris, you know when you told me I had to decide if the price was worth taking a stand?" he asked, as if I was too old to remember a conversation from two weeks prior.

I decided to humor him. "Yes, we talked about Character versus Reputation." I poured two cups of coffee and sat down at the dining room table across from him.

"Yes, that's right. So, I had to question if I would take a stand against my team's behaviors, or would I participate in expensing costs for that fancy dinner, which by the way was 2.5 times the per diem allowed by the company. Remember that I told you that before I left on the trip, I told everyone that we would only expense the amount the company per diem allowed and the rest we would pay as a personal expense?"

He's really making sure I did not forget a detail. I took a gulp of coffee before I made my point. "Yes, I do remember. You were teased by that one guy, and they didn't like you very much." I added to show him I was paying attention…and not that old.

"Well, they really didn't like me when I joined the company, but I always remember what you told me: 'It's better to be respected than liked in business.'"

So good to know my mentee pays attention too.

"That's right. You don't get paid for being liked; you get paid to perform a job. Stand up for your values. So…what happened?" Truly curious, this was like a joke being told by a two-year-old—you know, when you're wondering if we are ever going to get to a punch line.

"Well, I have a good relationship with the company's president. He doesn't like confrontation and is always concerned with people like me. Funny, huh?" He shot me a crooked smile.

Funny? No. You would be surprised to learn how many leaders avoid confrontation.

"It's not uncommon that leaders avoid confrontation, but it's necessary." I soft-pedaled my point, getting up to grab a plate of baked pastries.

"Well, before I left on the trip, I decided to take a stand like we talked about. I went into the president's office and told him about the dinner and that everyone was going. I also told him that

I explained to the team in a meeting that dinner would be over $100 a person and that we should only expense the $40 allowed by the company. Then I asked if everyone still wanted to go so I could make the update to the reservation if the number changed." He grabbed a miniature cinnamon roll and took a bite.

"What did he say?" Now I was leaning forward, 100% plus interested.

"He just laughed a little and said, 'Okay.' A bit dismissive, but I was okay with that. I wanted to have this interaction to reference should there be fallout from the dinner."

Boy, this one is smart—a preemptive strike.

"And was there? Any fallout?" I indulged him, as his demeanor when he walked in had already told me the answer.

He wiped a crumb from his lip before continuing. "Yes, but not in the way I had envisioned. After dinner, everyone wanted to go a club to go drinking. So, we went out to a bar with music and had drinks, and some went out on the dance floor. It was fun. We stayed out late and everyone definitely had a bit too much to drink. And, as we were leaving the bar, the club next door was just opening up and had a line forming outside. A couple of my team members went to the bouncer at the front of the line and tried to pay to cut in line and go into the club. I was over the limit as well, but when I saw the bouncer getting visibly irritated with my colleagues, I went up to see if I could help."

"And?"

Where is this going?

"The bouncer wanted nothing to do with any of us and was going to take action if we didn't leave, so we left," he said, as if the answer was obvious.

"I guess I am a little lost." I'm sure my forehead was scrunched with confusion.

"That's because I haven't told you the end of the story. Once we returned to the office, after about a week, the president asked to see me."

Am I wrong? Maybe his demeanor coming in didn't tell me how this played out.

"About what?" Nervous for my young mentee, I sat back in my chair.

"Well, apparently everyone on the trip had expensed the full amount of that dinner except me. He said he met with them to discuss it." There was no emotion in his voice.

Whoa! This can go in any direction.

"Did they try to defend it?" I asked.

"Sort of. They said we all decided to expense it 100%, including me. Then they told the president I was so drunk that I got everyone kicked out of a club that night." A wry smile spread across his face, like he was the only one in on the joke. He put cream in his coffee and took a drink.

"I thought you said your team didn't even get past the bouncer."

"Exactly!" He exclaimed as if he had presented the smoking gun as evidence in a murder trial.

"Continue! I am dying to hear how this ends!" I slid forward on my chair.

"The president told them that if there was anybody on the trip that would get the team kicked out of the club, I would be his last guess." He laughed.

"Funny, so that pre-emptive strike conversation about expensing the dinner paid off in a good way?" I stated the obvious.

"Yes, he said he only called me in to let me know what happened, so if people were behaving differently, not to worry about it because he wasn't. He really appreciated that I took a stand and cared about the company." You couldn't tell by how broad his shoulders were that he was wearing a sports jersey and not a 3-piece business suit.

"You stood up for something. That's character. And you didn't fall for their poor tactics, which would have hurt your reputation." I said, realizing I could not feel any prouder of this one.

"That's right. What did you always tell me? 'Character is what you stand for; Reputation is what you fall for.'"

He gets it!

"Or don't fall for, as this case has proven. I wouldn't be too worried about your coworkers. They will come around to appreciate you for the right reasons. Like being someone they can count on."

"I know. I am not too worried. Thanks, Aunt Kris, for always being there to help me." He popped the rest of his cinnamon roll in his mouth and stood to leave.

"Anytime. I am always here for you."

With a sweet smile and nod, he was gone.

CONCLUSION
20 YEARS LATER...

THE HOTEL'S CONFERENCE room was packed. Colleagues with whom I had formed a special bond during our experiences together at HCE were reuniting, and the combination of enthusiastic greetings between old friends and music was overwhelming and near deafening.

As I stood inside the door and watched people hug and share pictures of their families, I wondered, *Have we all been longing for the same special and unique experience we enjoyed while working at HCE? Those were some of the best years of my life...for so many reasons.*

"Kristin, there you are!" Cate exclaimed as she placed a glass of white wine in my hand and leaned in for a hug.

We toasted "cheers" and took a small sip.

She remembers I like an oaky chardonnay.

I noticed that she had hardly aged since that day I'd met her for breakfast at the Fairmont Hotel twenty years before. That same dark chestnut hair cut in a short bob style, with just a kiss of make-up and blush lip gloss.

Some looks are timeless.

"Cate, how are you? I can't believe it's been so long since we have seen each other. We promised last time we wouldn't let that happen again." The small growl in my tummy told me I should find some food.

"I know. It's just that life happens, right?" She scrunched her nose to emphasize her frustration with the pace of life that kept us apart.

"That's right, and I am teasing. I am just as responsible for not picking up the phone or shooting off an email." I shook my head a little.

Smelling the stuffed mushrooms being passed by cocktail servers, I noticed my hunger again and became slightly distracted while Cate continued talking.

"Kristin, don't you agree?" she asked, as I placed some of the appetizers in my napkin.

I turned my attention back to her in time to hear her repeat the question. "Kristin, I was saying, 'Don't you agree? Even though it has been years since we saw each other, it seems like yesterday; and we always pick up right where we left off.'"

"That is so true. Remember when we met at the Fairmont so many years ago, and you were so stressed out about what to do with your boyfriend, Ben?" I asked as soon as I finished savoring the delicious appetizer.

"Oh yes. That conversation, and many more during which you shared your advice and your mom's wisdom, have helped me make the right life decisions. I broke up with Ben after that trip and wrote down what I did and didn't want in life, and everything began to shift."

"Yes, clarity is a great map for life." I nodded in agreement as I waved over another server with small egg rolls. Securing a napkin with the hand my wine glass was in, I dipped the roll in sweet chili sauce and turned it over so the sauce dripped down the side.

"I was clear I wanted a family with a fully participating partner. I knew when I met Noah two years later that he was the one because our values and desires were aligned."

"I remember that call when you were first dating. I could tell from the tone in your voice how happy you were, and I can see on your face that you still are." I smiled at her happy glow.

"Yes, marriage is never 50/50, right? At least I know the goal is balance over time. That's why I decided, as difficult a decision it was, that leaving HCE was the right decision when we started the family."

"You still have a challenging and rewarding career as a professor, don't you?" I asked.

I wonder if she is happy with her choice.

"Yes, I love university life, and it works for me personally to get personal enrichment and have time for the family. I always dreamed of teaching, so I just moved it up my timeline when I realized it allows me 'have it all' without sacrificing so much time on the road like I did when we were at HCE."

"Talk about being road warriors, right? Speaking of having it all, let me see some pics of those kiddos. I can't wait for the family holiday card."

As she pulled out her smart phone, she paused for a moment and looked me straight in the eyes. "Kristin, I don't know if I ever told you, but I really do appreciate all the friendship and support you have given me over the years. I am sure you have helped countless others, but you've made a huge impact in my life."

She has no idea how much she and others have contributed to the richness that is my life.

"I've loved every minute of our chats, Cate. And yes, I've earned the title of 'Aunt Kris' in every work environment I've been in, and have just recently decided to create a personal brand to help more young professionals."

"Really? That sounds amazing. But how will you have enough time for all of those coffee breaks, phone calls, and meals?" she asked, half joking and half serious.

I must keep the meals—maybe "Cooking with Aunt Kris"?

I laughed with her before answering, "My plan is to create an online platform where I can mentor larger groups, and I will probably host some small retreats and coaching programs as well for those who really want to create success quickly. And of course, there will be delicious food!" I raised an eyebrow, quietly requesting her feedback.

She got the message quickly and filled my heart to capacity with her response: "Wow, I would have jumped on that opportunity in two seconds when I was in the early stages of my career. What an amazing idea! Those young professionals are lucky to have you, *Aunt Kris*." She emphasized my branded name, smiling at the ring of it.

I took a deep breath as I felt the excitement expand in my chest and then turned my attention back to her cell phone.

"Thank you, Cate. Now, show me those pics—I can't wait to see how your kids have grown."

Wow, what a beautiful family.

ABOUT
AUNT KRIS

KRISTIN WILLIAMS, PRESIDENT MNK Engagement, is a Mentor, Sponsor, Trainer, Generational Workplace Guide, Speaker, and Coach who helps young professionals acquire the ingredients they need to cook up a successful personal and professional life. As the last of 6 siblings, she reaped the deep wisdom of parents who were committed to personal and professional growth. She's also a wife, a sister, and an aunt to 20 nieces and nephews and 20 grand-nieces and -nephews who rely on her for solid advice in business, relationships, finances, cooking, and so much more.

As a Pepperdine University graduate of one of the first behavioral business programs, she started her career understanding the power of relationships and found success quite rapidly. Her career in technology, with the leading technology publisher, allowed her to witness firsthand some of the business world's most pivotal occurrences during the technology boom of the 90's. She had a front row seat in the boardrooms of some of America's most notable organizations today. Having weathered many societal shifts in the workplace as a young professional, she understands the personal journey and its challenges and has mentored hundreds of other young professionals.

A food enthusiast and home chef, Kristin knows that a good recipe can take time to perfect, and decided to launch the "Aunt Kris" brand to help young professionals work on finding their unique recipe for their best life. She enjoys 1-to-1 mentoring and now facilitates intimate online communities and in-person retreats for young professionals to build relationships, climb the corporate ladder, and create a truly delicious life. Plus, it's a fun way for her to model what she teaches—creating a life that simultaneously combines her love of mentoring, cooking, and traveling.

Kristin is the 2017 Honoree Employer Partner for Youth Employment Services (Y.E.S.) Mentor Award and an Inaugural Member of Forbes Council on Human Resources.

She resides in California with the love of her life and husband, a professor in the Cal State University system.

JOIN THE FAMILY

If you are ready to get noticed and get ahead
and want the inside scoop on the ingredients you'll need to do it…

If you know you learn more quickly and thoroughly
while working with mentors and peers…

If you want access and support through the process
of whipping up delicious success in all areas of your life…

Our family is the place to be.

Head over to AuntKris.com

Sign Up to Develop Your Personal Brand Plan

and

Claim Your Place in Our Family
[and be the first to receive invitations to
workshops and retreats!]

www.AuntKris.com
www.Facebook.com/AskAuntKris